Parent Pains

Darrell
Pearson

Marv
Penner

David C. Cook Publishing Co.
Elgin, Illinois—Weston, Ontario

Custom Curriculum
Parent Pains

Unless otherwise noted, Scripture quotations are from the Holy Bible, New International Version (NIV), © 1973, 1978, 1984 by International Bible Society. Used by permission of Zondervan Bible Publishers.

Published by David C. Cook Publishing Co.
850 North Grove Ave., Elgin, IL 60120
Cable address: DCCOOK
Series creator: John Duckworth
Series editor: Randy Southern
Editor: Randy Southern
Option writers: Randy Southern, Nelson E. Copeland, Jr., and Ellen Larson
Designer: Bill Paetzold
Cover illustrator: Ned Shaw
Inside illustrator: John Hayes
Printed in U.S.A.

ISBN: 0-7814-4999-5

CONTENTS

Sessions by Marv Penner
Options by Randy Southern, Nelson E. Copeland, Jr., and Ellen Larson

About the Authors

Marv Penner is a veteran youth worker and seminar leader. He is also chairman of the counseling department at Briercrest Schools in Saskatchewan, Canada.

Randy Southern is an editor of youth products in the Church Ministries division of David C. Cook. He has also written several books including *It Came from the Media* and *Cross Training* (SonPower).

Nelson E. Copeland, Jr. is a nationally known speaker and the author of several youth resources including *Great Games for City Kids* (Youth Specialties) and *A New Agenda for Urban Youth* (Winston-Derek). He is president of the Christian Education Coalition for African-American Leadership (CECAAL), an organization dedicated to reinforcing educational and cultural excellence among urban teenagers. He also serves as youth pastor at the First Baptist Church in Morton, Pennsylvania.

Ellen Larson is an educator and writer with degrees in education and theology. She has served as minister of Christian education in several churches, teaching teens and children, as well as their teachers. Her experience also includes teaching in public schools. She is the author of several books for Christian education teachers, and frequently leads training seminars for volunteer teachers. Ellen and her husband live in San Diego and are the parents of two daughters.

You've Made the Right Choice!

Thanks for choosing **Custom Curriculum**! We think your choice says at least three things about you:

(1) You know your group pretty well, and want your program to fit that group like a glove;

(2) You like having options instead of being boxed in by some far-off curriculum editor;

(3) You have a small mole on your left forearm, exactly two inches above the elbow.

OK, so we were wrong about the mole. But if you like having choices that help you tailor meetings to fit your kids, **Custom Curriculum** *is* the best place to be.

Going through Customs

In this (and every) **Custom Curriculum** volume, you'll find
- five great sessions you can use anytime, in any order.
- reproducible student handouts, at least one per session.
- a truckload of options for adapting the sessions to your group (more about that in a minute).
- a helpful get-you-ready article by a youth expert.
- clip art for making posters, fliers, and other kinds of publicity to get kids to your meetings.

Each **Custom Curriculum** session has three to six steps. No matter how many steps a session has, it's designed to achieve these goals:

- *Getting together.* Using an icebreaker activity, you'll help kids be glad they came to the meeting.

- *Getting thirsty.* Why should kids care about your topic? Why should they care what the Bible has to say about it? You'll want to take a few minutes to earn their interest before you start pouring the "living water."

- *Getting the Word.* By exploring and discussing carefully selected passages, you'll find out what God has to say.

- *Getting the point.* Here's where you'll help kids make the leap from principles to nitty-gritty situations they are likely to face.

- *Getting personal.* What should each group member do as a result of this session? You'll help each person find a specific "next-step" response that works for him or her.

Each session is written to last 45 to 60 minutes. But what if you have less time—or more? No problem! **Custom Curriculum** is all about ... options!

What Are My Options?

Every **Custom Curriculum** session gives you fourteen kinds of options:

• *Extra Action*—for groups that learn better when they're physically moving (instead of just reading, writing, and discussing).

• *Combined Junior High/High School*—to use when you're mixing age levels, and an activity or case study would be too "young" or "old" for part of the group.

• *Small Group*—for adapting activities that would be tough with groups of fewer than eight kids.

• *Large Group*—to alter steps for groups of more than twenty kids.

• *Urban*—for fitting sessions to urban facilities and multiethnic (especially African-American) concerns.

• *Heard It All Before*—for fresh approaches that get past the defenses of kids who are jaded by years in church.

• *Little Bible Background*—to use when most of your kids are strangers to the Bible, or haven't made a Christian commitment.

• *Mostly Guys*—to focus on guys' interests and to substitute activities they might be more enthused about.

• *Mostly Girls*—to address girls' concerns and to substitute activities they might prefer.

• *Extra Fun*—for longer, more "rowdy" youth meetings where the emphasis is on fun.

• *Short Meeting Time*—tips for condensing the session to 30 minutes or so.

• *Fellowship & Worship*—for building deeper relationships or enabling kids to praise God together.

• *Media*—to spice up meetings with video, music, or other popular media.

• *Sixth Grade*—appearing only in junior high/middle school volumes, this option helps you change steps that sixth graders might find hard to understand or relate to.

• *Extra Challenge*—appearing only in high school volumes, this option lets you crank up the voltage for kids who are ready for more Scripture or more demanding personal application.

Each kind of option is offered twice in each session. So in this book, you get *almost 150* ways to tweak the meetings to fit your group!

Customizing a Session

All right, you may be thinking. *With all of these options flying around, how do I put a session together? I don't have a lot of time, you know.*

We know! That's why we've made **Custom Curriculum** as easy to follow as possible. Let's take a look at how you might prepare an actual meeting. You can do that in four easy steps:

(1) *Read the basic session plan.* Start by choosing one or more of the goals listed at the beginning of the session. You have three to pick from: a goal that emphasizes *knowledge,* one that stresses *understanding,* and one that emphasizes *action.* Choose one or more, depending on what *you* want to accomplish. Then read the basic plan to see what will work for you and what might not.

(2) *Choose your options.* You don't *have* to use any options at all; the

basic session plan would work well for many groups, and you may want to stick with it if you have absolutely no time to consider options. But if you want a more perfect fit, check out your choices.

As you read the basic session plan, you'll see small symbols in the margin. Each symbol stands for a different kind of option. When you see a symbol, it means that kind of option is offered for that step. Turn to the page noted by the symbol and you'll see that option explained.

Let's say you have a small group, mostly guys who get bored if they don't keep moving. You'll want to keep an eye out for three kinds of options: Small Group, Mostly Guys, and Extra Action. As you read the basic session, you might spot symbols that tell you there are Small Group options for Step 1 and Step 3—maybe a different way to play a game so that you don't need big teams, and a way to cover several Bible passages when just a few kids are looking them up. Then you see symbols telling you that there are Mostly Guys options for Step 2 and Step 4—perhaps a substitute activity that doesn't require too much self-disclosure, and a case study guys will relate to. Finally you see symbols indicating Extra Action options for Step 2 and Step 3—maybe an active way to get kids' opinions instead of handing out a survey, and a way to act out some verses instead of just looking them up.

After reading the options, you might decide to use four of them. You base your choices on your personal tastes and the traits of your group that you think are most important right now. **Custom Curriculum** offers you more options than you'll need, so you can pick your current favorites and plug others into future meetings if you like.

(3) *Use the checklist.* Once you've picked your options, keep track of them with the simple checklist that appears at the end of each option section (just before the start of the next session plan). This little form gives you a place to write down the materials you'll need too—since they depend on the options you've chosen.

(4) *Get your stuff together.* Gather your materials; photocopy any Repro Resources (reproducible student sheets) you've decided to use. And . . . you're ready!

The Custom Curriculum Challenge

Your kids are fortunate to have you as their leader. You see them not as a bunch of generic teenagers, but as real, live, unique kids. You care whether you really connect with them. That's why you're willing to take a few extra minutes to tailor your meetings to fit.

It's a challenge to work with real, live kids, isn't it? We think you deserve a standing ovation for taking that challenge. And we pray that **Custom Curriculum** helps you shape sessions that shape lives for Jesus Christ and His kingdom.

—*The Editors*

Talking to Junior Highers about Parent Pains

by Darrell Pearson

It was 4:45 on a Monday afternoon. The office seemed unbearably hot. I was tired from a long ministry weekend. And yet here I sat in the most dreaded of situations.

I was counseling a mother and her teenage son.

Maybe some youth workers enjoy such situations, but I've always found them to be very taxing on my life and ministry. Some call it "hopeless" counseling. It's not like the joy of premarital counseling with an infatuated couple. Instead, there's a sadness in talking with a motivated mom and a disinterested kid. It's discouraging, frustrating, and tiring.

But it's good. The more I talked with the two of them, the more I realized that, with me present, they were able to do what was impossible by themselves. They could *talk*.

Is there a more helpful role that the youth leader plays in this world than helping bridge the gap between parents and their teenagers? Probably not. Above all, we are often mediators between people caught in a classic struggle. But we can make a difference.

The sessions that follow will help you as you work with students trying to understand and communicate with their parents. I thought a few guidelines about the parent-child situation as it pertains to a youth worker might help, so the next few paragraphs are thoughts, principles, ideas, and suggestions to make your role more productive.

You Are an Extension of the Parents.

Face it: You're an adult. You *look* like a parent, you *act* like one (most of the time)—you might even *be* a parent. And the parents of your group members have entrusted you with the care of their children (even if that care extends only for a few hours a week). Many of these parents probably have strong expectations that you're going to deliver the same message that they would deliver if they were working with these kids.

Sometimes you might live up to these expectations; sometimes you might not. Either way, you need to remember your role. Whatever you teach your group members needs to be delivered from the perspective of an adult, a person who generally supports what the parents are doing.

It's not helpful to play the role of the "teenage sympathizer," who sees everything from the kid's point of view. You may be the closest thing to a parent some of your group members have. And with the credibility you most likely have with your group members, the parents need to be comfortable that you're a trustworthy person with whom to leave their sons or daughters for a while.

Parents Don't Own Their Children.

On the other hand, you can't play the parents' role only in the way parents want. Junior highers are not puppets of their parents. They are distinct individuals who deserve to be treated as such. (Remember, not all parents treat their children well.) Part of your mediator role is understanding that you won't always side with the parents. You must be willing to take a stand sometimes to support the kids' perspectives. Parents don't *own* their children; they are entrusted by God to take care of *His* children, just as they entrust you to do the same.

Communicating with Parents Is Critical to Your Ministry.

It's an unwise youth leader who purposely steps on parents' toes to make friends with students. Parents are the lifeblood of your existence—so take steps to make sure you treat them like VIPs. Communicate accurately with them, listen to their concerns, and respond to them. A lot of youth ministry involves "parent ministry."

Since you're about to embark on a study about parents, why not take a moment to write a note to parents to tell them what you're about to do? They'll greatly appreciate the information. Perhaps they'll want to quiz their junior highers about the sessions in the series. Invite parents to drop in for a meeting, or perhaps include them in a panel discussion. *Involve* them in the process and you'll be amazed at how many of them are willing to help.

You Are "Jeremiah" to Parents and Teens.

The Old Testament prophets often found themselves in an uncomfortable role—challenging wayward people with the true claims of the living God. It often got them in deep trouble, but it brought people into a closer relationship with God. Playing the "prophet" with parents and teens can be a big help to them as they seek to grow together in their relationships with Christ and with each other. When group members raise concerns about parents (particularly unfair concerns) during your meeting, carefully challenge kids to consider the other side of the problem. Find creative ways to explore this. For instance, you might have a "guest" parent in your group show up to answer questions or roleplay the parental perspective. You'll also need to be prepared to challenge parents, too, when they need to be confronted.

Parents and Teens See Things from Their Own Perspective.

Both parents and teens believe their perspective to be completely accurate. When one tells you his or her side of a story, you think you know every detail and truth that's needed. But you don't.

When a mom recently came to me to explain her family's problems, I thought I had an accurate picture of what was going on. When I talked to the daughter, however, she gave me a whole new perspective. After my conversation with the daughter, I thought I knew what was *really* happening, so I made a few judgmental comments about the mom to the daughter. The mom then came back to me to see if what her daughter had said I said was true, and . . . you get the picture. When I talked to both of them together, I formed a *third* opinion of the situation. Be careful not to trust one side or the other too much for truth. Every individual is convinced that he or she sees the whole issue accurately. Don't be swayed by a convincing argument, but instead by your own observations and feelings after exploring the issue as completely as you can.

Don't Be Defensive about the Parent Role.

This is especially easy to do if you are a parent yourself. It's understandable to feel defensive when a junior higher makes an outlandish remark about his or her parents, but allow the person to vent his or her feelings and opinions. A youth group meeting, Bible study, or Sunday school class is a perfect place for kids to talk about parents without feeling like they have to hold things back. A defensive response on your part will just cause them to shut up and stop sharing. As you discuss the topic of parents, fight the urge to "defend the parental flag"; instead, be willing to listen with an open mind.

Talking with junior highers about parent pains is no easy task. In John 9, the Pharisees found themselves in the midst of an interesting parent-son issue. The blind man that Jesus healed was summoned by the Pharisees to explain what happened, and when he failed to satisfy them, they called in his parents. The parents' only comment was that their son was old enough to speak for himself. Their interest was in themselves—they just didn't want to get in trouble with anyone, and didn't seem to care much about the fact that their blind son was healed.

Such is life with young people and parents even today. Many teens and parents are motivated by self-interest, so healing wounds between the parties doesn't happen easily. But Jesus can and will heal people and relationships today—and He can use us to help do it. We can be instrumental in bridging the gap between parents and junior highers. Let's do a better job than the Pharisees did, and put our own self-interest aside, trying our best to help our group members understand and live with their parents.

Darrell Pearson is co-founder of 10 to 20, an organization dedicated to presenting high-involvement events for teenagers. Formerly youth director at the First Presbyterian Church in Colorado Springs, Darrell spent most of his eleven years there directing the junior high program. He's co-authored Creative Programming Ideas for Junior High Ministry *(Youth Specialties), and written and presented the national-touring program* Next Exit. *He also speaks frequently to youth groups and leaders around the country. He lives with his wife and three daughters in Colorado Springs, Colorado.*

The images on these two pages are designed to help you promote this course within your church and community. Feel free to photocopy anything here and adapt it to fit your publicity needs. The stuff on this page could be used as a flier that you send or hand out to kids—or as a bulletin insert. The stuff on the next page could be used to add visual interest to newsletters, calendars, bulletin boards, or other promotions. Be creative and have fun!

Ever Feel Like Your Parents Are a Pain?

If you've ever had trouble loving or even understanding your parents, please join us as we begin a new study called *Parent Pains*. You'll be glad you did—and so will your parents!

Who:

When:

Where:

Questions? Call:

Parent Pains

Parent Pains

Follow the rules.

For kids only.

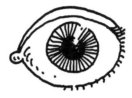

Most Valuable Parents

Did you hear me?

Living with Imperfect Parents

Choose one or more

- ☐ To help kids recognize that most parents are at least somewhat aware of their weaknesses and really want to be better parents.

- ☐ To help kids understand that their shortcomings are every bit as responsible for family problems as their parents' shortcomings are.

- ☐ To help kids feel secure in the fact that they have a heavenly Father who can consistently provide what they need, even when their earthly parents fail them.

- ☐ Other _____

Your Bible Base:

Psalm 27:10
Matthew 7:1-5

Building the Perfect Parent

(Needed: Cut-apart copies of Repro Resource 1, chalkboard and chalk or newsprint and marker)

Ask: **How many of you have ever wished you had parents other than the ones you have now?** If group members seem hesitant to answer, rephrase the question: **How many of you have ever wished you could change some things about your parents?** Probably most of your group members have wished this at one time or another. To "break the ice," you might want to share something about your parents that, when you were younger, you wished you could change about them.

Then ask: **If you could create the ideal parents, what would they be like? What attributes would you give them? What are the most important traits good parents should have?** Get responses from as many group members as possible.

Before the session, you'll need to cut apart copies of "Parent Traits" (Repro Resource 1). Distribute one set of cards from Repro Resource 1 and a pencil to each group member. Instruct group members to arrange the cards according to how important they think each parent trait is. (There are a couple of blank cards provided in case group members want to write down some parent traits of their own.) For instance, if they think being wealthy is the most important trait a parent can have, they should put the "Wealthy" card first. If they think being laid-back is the least important trait a parent can have, they should put the "Laid-back" card last.

Give group members a few minutes to work. When everyone is finished, have each group member read aloud his or her top three parent traits. Keep a tally on the board of group members' responses.

Then ask several volunteers to explain why they chose the traits they did as being important. Note which group members chose superficial qualities (like being wealthy, good-looking, well-dressed, etc.) as being important and which group members chose "deeper" qualities (like being forgiving, patient, and understanding).

Keep in mind that many of your group members may come from single-parent families or families in which they're not experiencing healthy parenting. For some of them, just thinking about the qualities of a great parent will be a painful exercise. Be sensitive to this.

OPTIONS

EXTRA ACTION

SMALL GROUP

LARGE GROUP

HEARD IT ALL BEFORE

MOSTLY GIRLS

MOSTLY GUYS

EXTRA FUN

MEDIA

JR. HIGH HIGH SCHOOL COMBINED

STEP 2

Top Ten Parent Pains

(Needed: A large sheet of newsprint or poster board with graffiti written on it, tape, markers, index cards, pencils)

Before the session, you'll need to prepare a large sheet of newsprint or poster board. Write some of the following statements "graffiti-style" on the sheet.
- "My parents don't trust me."
- "My mom sees only my mistakes."
- "My parents have unreasonable expectations."
- "My dad is too busy for me."

The statements should be scattered randomly across the sheet. However, make sure you leave plenty of space on the sheet for more comments to be added later.

At this point of the session, bring out the sheet and tape it to the wall. Distribute markers to your group members. Explain to them that the newsprint or poster board on the wall is a graffiti sheet for "parent pains"—things about parents that upset or irritate their kids. Then have group members come up to the sheet and add their own parent pains.

After a few minutes, have group members take their seats. Briefly go through the parent pains they wrote down, allowing group members to comment on each one. Probably most of the comments you'll get will be ones of hearty agreement.

Distribute an index card and a pencil to each group member. Instruct group members to create their own "top ten lists" of parent pains—the things about *their* parents that upset or irritate *them*.

Group members may choose from the "pains" written on the graffiti sheet or they may add some of their own. They should list the pains in reverse order—from #10 to #1 (with #10 being the least irritating or upsetting and #1 being the most irritating or upsetting).

When everyone is finished, have group members form teams of three or four and read their lists to each other. Walk among the teams as group members share their lists. Pay attention to the parent pains they identify as being most irritating or upsetting.

Afterward, say: **It seems like we put up with a lot of "parent pains," doesn't it? But what if the tables were turned? What if we had your parents in here, listing their top ten "kid complaints"? What do you suppose their top complaints would be?** Most group members will probably give answers like not cleaning up their rooms, watching too much TV, not taking care of their stuff, fighting with their brothers and sisters, etc. [NOTE: Some group members may give more serious, disturbing answers like "My parents complain that I'm too stupid" or "My parents complain because they don't want me around." You may want to offer to meet with these young people after the session to discuss their problems at home more thoroughly.]

STEP 3

Family Log Jams

(Needed: Copies of Repro Resource 2, pencils)

OPTIONS

HEARD IT ALL BEFORE

LITTLE BIBLE BACKGROUND

SHORT MEETING TIME

SIXTH GRADE

Say: **When we have conflict at home with our parents, it's pretty easy to spot the things they are doing wrong. It's not always so easy to spot our own faults.**

Have someone read aloud Matthew 7:1-5. Then ask: **What does Jesus mean when He says to "take the plank out of your own eye" before you "remove the speck" from someone else's eye?** (Before you start confronting others about their faults, you should work on your own faults.)

Why is it so much easier to recognize other people's faults than it is to recognize our own faults? Get responses from as many group members as possible.

How does it make you feel when other people see only your faults and fail to recognize your good points? Again get responses from as many group members as possible.

Say: **When we have problems with our parents, it's like we create a "log jam" in our families. Very little positive communication or healthy interaction can get through the log jam. Unfortunately, blaming our parents for the problems doesn't get rid of the log jams. We have to focus on our own faults as well.**

Distribute copies of "Log Jam!" (Repro Resource 2) and pencils. Give group members a few minutes to complete the sheets. When everyone is finished, ask volunteers to share some of their responses.

Then ask: **How might the things you identified about yourself contribute to log jams in your family?** Get several responses.

Ask group members to keep these sheets handy and refer to them when they notice "log jams" in their families. Encourage them to take the first step in eliminating the log jams by working on the faults they identified on the sheet.

Parenting 101

(Needed: Chalkboard and chalk or newsprint and marker)

Ask: **Did you know that every day you are learning some valuable lessons about how to be an effective parent? By watching your own parents, you're learning good things that you'll put into practice and bad things that you'll avoid later on in your lives when you have kids of your own.**

What are some things you've learned from your parents that you want to make sure to do just like them when you get to be parents? What are some things about your parents' styles that you're going to make sure to eliminate from your lives when you become parents?

Make two lists on the board and write down group members' responses as they are given. You might use the following headings for the lists: "Things about My Parents I'd Like to Copy" and "Things about My Parents I'd Rather Not Copy."

Try to emphasize the positive things group members identify about their parents. In doing so, you may help eliminate some bad attitudes group members have toward their parents. On the other hand, don't ignore group members' negative comments. It's important for kids to have an understanding adult hear some of their complaints. Try to bring some mature balance and wisdom to your group members' enthusiastic evaluations.

One Perfect Father

Say: **Today we've discovered that the people we call parents are less than perfect. For some of you, this might come as a surprise. Others of you may have already made this discovery. Like all human beings, parents have flaws and make mistakes.**

Have group members refer to the top ten "parent pains" lists they made earlier. Then say: **I know that many of you are a little disappointed when you think about mistakes your parents have made in raising you. But let's not end our time on a depressing note. I have some good news for you from God's Word.**

Have someone read aloud Psalm 27:10. Explain: **This verse tells us that even if our parents were to make the biggest mistake of all and completely abandon us** (be aware that for some kids this is a reality), **we have a heavenly Father who will always be there for us!**

Give group members an opportunity to silently thank God for His consistent love and to pray for their parents in the tough job they have of being moms and dads.

PARENT TRAITS

WEALTHY	EXPRESSIVE (often hugs me, kisses me, and says "I love you")	LAID BACK
GOOD SENSE OF HUMOR	GOOD-LOOKING	FORGIVING
CONCERNED ABOUT ME	LIKES MY FRIENDS	LIKED BY MY FRIENDS
ALLOWS ME TO BE INDEPENDENT	PATIENT	UNDERSTANDING
WELL-RESPECTED IN THE COMMUNITY	YOUNG	ATHLETIC/ PHYSICALLY FIT
WELL-DRESSED		

Log Jam!

One rule in my house that's often hard for me to obey is

A habit I have that sometimes annoys my family is

Of all of my assigned chores, the one I forget to do most often is

Something I often forget to say "thank you" to my family for is

One area of my attitude that could use some improvement is

Step 1

Before the session, list the parent traits on Repro Resource 1 according to how important *you* think each one is (with #1 being the most important and #16 being the least important). Don't let any group members see your list. To begin the session, form two teams. Have the teams line up behind a start/finish line. Place two sets of cards from Repro Resource 1 on the floor on the other side of the room. When you say go, the first person for each team will run to his or her team's set of cards, arrange them according to how he or she thinks you listed them, and run back. You will then check the order of the cards against your list and mark the ones that are in the correct position. Then the second person in line will attempt to arrange the rest of the cards in the "correct" order. Continue until one team correctly lists all of its cards. Afterward, have group members comment on your list. Do they agree with the order in which you placed the traits? Point out that everyone has different ideas about what traits are important for parents to have.

Step 2

Rather than having group members write down their parents' top kid complaints, ask volunteers to do impressions of their parents' complaining. They can mimic their parents' voice, appearance, mannerisms, facial expressions, and "pet phrases." Encourage volunteers not to be mean-spirited in their impressions. You may want to set the tone for the activity by doing an impression of one of your parents. If your group members are hesitant to "perform" in front of the group, try another approach. Call out some typical parental complaints; instruct group members to jump to their feet if their parents have ever had similar complaints. Among the complaints you might use are not cleaning your room, watching too much TV, not doing assigned chores, talking back, and picking on your brother or sister.

Step 1

As a group, build the "perfect" parent. Have each person call out a characteristic of a perfect parent. These might include things like patience, forgiveness, understanding, love, etc. Write the characteristics on the board as they are named. Then have group members decide what kind of job a perfect parent would have, what kind of car he or she would drive, where he or she would live, what he or she would do in his or her spare time, etc. Afterward, discuss the downfalls of the various characteristics. For instance, if a parent had a job that required a lot of travel, he or she wouldn't be able to see his or her kids' ballgames and school activities. Point out that there is no such thing as a perfect parent. All parents have good points and bad points.

Step 4

Rather than having group members list things about their parents they would and wouldn't like to copy, take advantage of your group's smallness by having members form pairs. Instruct the members of each pair to come up with two (one per person) brief roleplays demonstrating what they'd like to copy about their parents. For instance, if one member of a pair appreciated his father's encouraging nature, he might come up with a roleplay in which the father is encouraging his son after a tough loss in a basketball game. After all the pairs have presented their roleplays, discuss as a group some parental characteristics your group members *wouldn't* like to copy.

Step 1

Depending on the size of your group, have group members form ten to sixteen teams. (A "team" may be as small as two people.) Give each team one of the "parent trait" cards from Repro Resource 1. There are sixteen cards you could use; if you have fewer than sixteen teams, choose the cards that seem most applicable to your group members' families. Give the teams two or three minutes to come up with explanations for why their assigned parent trait is the most important trait a parent could have. (Group members don't actually have to *believe* that their trait is most important; they just have to come up with a convincing argument for it.) After a few minutes, have each team make its presentation. You may want to award a prize to the team with the most convincing argument. Afterward, discuss as a group which parent traits are *really* important.

Step 5

Use the anonymity of your large group to your advantage as you wrap up the session. Have someone read aloud Psalm 27:10. Point out that not only is our heavenly Father always there for us, He is also willing and able to help us with problems we have with our earthly parents. Distribute index cards and pencils. Instruct your group members to write down one problem they have with their parents that they'd like God's help with. Group members should *not* write their names on the cards. As you collect and shuffle the cards, have group members form teams of four. Distribute four index cards to each team, and instruct the members of each team to pray together for the requests written on the cards.

Step 1

On the two blank "parent trait" cards on Repro Resource 1, write the following traits: "Concerned about my spiritual life/church attendance" and "Allows me to believe and worship however I choose to." Distribute the cards and have group members rank them according to how important they think each one is. Afterward, focus your discussion on the two traits you wrote earlier. Find out how much influence parents have on your group members' beliefs and church attendance/involvement. Use the following questions as needed to guide your discussion.

• **On a scale of 1 to 10, how concerned would you say your parents are about your spiritual life? How does that make you feel?**
• **If your parents gave you the freedom to believe and worship as you choose, how would it affect your church attendance? How would it affect your involvement with this group?**

Step 3

In discussing Matthew 7:1-5 with kids who've "heard it all before," use the following questions.

• **When do we have the right to point out another person's faults and weaknesses?** (When our motive is love or concern for the person.)
• **After having read Matthew 7:1-5, would you say we have the right to point out our parents' faults and weaknesses? If so, under what conditions?** Get opinions from as many group members as possible.

Step 3

If your group members aren't familiar with Scripture, they may be confused by Jesus' use of figurative language in Matthew 7:1-5. As a group, brainstorm some modern-day figures of speech or expressions that might be confusing to people two thousand years from now. Among the suggestions you might come up with are "Excellent!" (from *Wayne's World*); "Get off my back"; "Chill"; "Hasta la vista, baby"; etc. Point out that Jesus was communicating in terms His immediate audience (His first-century followers) would understand. Have your group members brainstorm some modern ways to express the "Judge not, lest you be judged" message of Matthew 7:1-5.

Step 5

As you wrap up the session, distribute index cards to your group members. Have them write down the following Scripture passages: Psalm 139:7-12; Matthew 28:20; and Hebrews 13:5. Explain that these are other verses of assurance that the Lord will always be there for us. In addition to the references themselves, group members should write down the page numbers in their Bibles where these verses are found. Encourage group members to look up these passages when they feel ignored or neglected by their parents.

Step 4

Turn over the sheet of newsprint or poster board you used for the graffiti exercise in Step 2 (or use a new sheet). Write at the top of the sheet "Here's why I'm thankful to You, Lord, for my parents." Then distribute markers and have your group members write at least one thing they're thankful for concerning their parents. Comments may include the following:
• "My parents care enough about me to worry when I get home later than I'm supposed to."
• "My parents say my friends are always welcome at our house."
• "My parents bought me a puppy after my dog died."
Encourage group members not to just write down something nice about their parents, but to direct their comments to God and to thank *Him* for their parents.

Step 5

Distribute index cards and pencils. Instruct group members to pair up, preferably with a friend (or at least someone they're comfortable with). Have them share with their partners one thing about their relationship with their parents that they'd like their partners to pray about in the coming week. It might be something as specific as "Please pray that my parents will let me go to the basketball game on Friday instead of making me go to my cousin's birthday party." Or it might be something as general as "Please pray that my mom and I will stop arguing so much." Group members should write down their partners' requests on the index cards and keep the cards handy as prayer reminders. To begin next week's session, have the partners pair up and update each other.

MOSTLY GIRLS

Step 1

After you've made a tally of the top three parent traits, ask the girls to read aloud the three traits that they considered *least* important. Make a tally of these traits and discuss some of the reasons these things don't seem very important. Ask: **Have some of you put too much emphasis on some qualities that really aren't very important? How can seeing others' perspectives help you?**

Step 4

As the girls are talking about the lessons they're learning from their parents, ask them to name some frequent expressions used by one or both of their parents. Give them some examples, such as "If I've told you once, I've told you a million times ...," "When I was your age ...," and "It doesn't matter why, I just said to do it!" List group members' responses on the board and then talk about the expressions. Ask: **Which of these expressions might have an element of truth? Do you often have to be reminded about things? Which ones are just results of frustration? How should you respond to these expressions? Which expressions do you think you will use when you're a parent? Why?**

MOSTLY GUYS

Step 1

Rather than having group members fill in the two blank cards on Repro Resource 1, fill them in yourself with the following traits: "Plays sports with me" and "Spends time with me." Explain that "Plays sports with me" includes things like a father throwing a football or baseball with his son in the back yard; a father taking his son golfing; a father teaching his son how to play basketball, soccer, or chess; etc. "Spends time with me" includes things like going out to dinner with a parent for "one-on-one time"; going to a ball game, movie, play, or concert together; etc. Afterward, discuss how important sports- and entertainment-related activities are in a father-son relationship.

Step 2

If you have guys in your group whose fathers don't live at home, ask them to write down some of the pains of being the "man of the house." (However, be sensitive as you do this! Make sure that you don't put anyone on the spot or embarrass anyone.) You might initiate this by writing some of the following statements on the graffiti sheet:
• "My mom expects me to watch my little brother/sister while she's at work."
• "If there's a spider or bug in the house, my mom always makes me kill it."
• "My mom makes me rake leaves in the fall, shovel snow in the winter, water the grass in the spring, and mow the lawn in the summer. She never makes my little brother do anything!"

EXTRA FUN

Step 1

A few days prior to the session, you'll need to take pictures (using instant-developing film, if possible) of three of your group members' parents. If it's a guy in your group, take a picture of his father; if it's a girl, take a picture of her mother. Also, if possible, bring to your meeting the clothes the parents were wearing in the pictures. You'll also need to bring makeup, disguise props (fake beards, mustaches, glasses, etc.), and hairstyling items (curling iron, gel, mousse, etc.). Have group members form three teams. Assign to each team one of the group members whose parent's picture was taken. Each team's goal is to make its assigned group member look as much like his or her parent as possible. Working with the photos as a guide, the teams will use the clothes and various costume supplies to do their make-overs. Give the teams several minutes to work. Afterward, hold a "fashion show" for each team to show off its work.

Step 2

Distribute paper and pencils to your group members. Write "Parents for Rent" on the board. Have group members imagine that they're going to rent out their parents for a week. Instruct your group members to write a classified ad that could appear in the "Parents for Rent" section of your local newspaper. (You may want to have some actual newspaper classified ads available for group members to refer to.) Encourage them to be truthful in their ads, identifying boths strengths and weaknesses of their parents in their ads. For instance, someone might write "Parents for rent. Father—hard working & strong, but often grouchy. Mother—loving & concerned (sometimes too concerned); also an experienced chauffeur." After each group member shares his or her ad, discuss as a group what kind of person might respond to the ad.

Step 1

Before the session, you'll need to record several video clips of various TV and movie personalities and characters. To begin the session, play the tape and have group members vote as to whether each character would be a good parent or a bad parent. Among the personalities and characters you might use are Ward and June Cleaver (from *Leave It to Beaver*), Mike and Carol Brady (from *The Brady Bunch*), Hulk Hogan (professional wrestler), Steve Urkel (from *Family Matters*), and Homer and Marge Simpson (from *The Simpsons*). After each vote, have several group members explain why they voted as they did. Encourage group members to be as creative and humorous as possible in their explanations. For instance, Hulk Hogan might be a good father because he could protect his children from bullies.

Step 2

If possible, without your group members' knowledge, record some of their parents complaining (good-naturedly) about their kids. Try to get the parents to give personal, but non-embarrassing, information about their kids in their complaints. (For example, one parent might say, "My son hasn't changed the water in the fishbowl in his room for so long that his goldfish is now a blackfish.") However, the parents should not mention their kids' names. Play the recording for your group members and have them guess whose parents are speaking.

Step 2

Instead of having group members come up to the board to write, have them call out their "parent pains," while you write them on the board. After you get about eight or nine suggestions, distribute index cards and pencils. Have group members choose their top *three* (as opposed to ten) parent pains and write them on the cards. Then, rather than having group members form teams to talk about their lists, ask volunteers to read their lists aloud. Pay attention to the pains they identify as being most irritating or upsetting.

Step 3

Rather than distributing Repro Resource 2 and waiting while group members fill it out, have volunteers call out answers to the following questions:
- **What's a rule at your house that's hard for you to obey?**
- **What's a habit you have that sometimes annoys your family?**
- **What chore or job around the house do you most often forget to do?**
- **What one thing do you most often forget to say thank you to your family for?**
- **What's one area of your attitude that could use some improvement?**

If your group members are hesitant to respond, you might want to be prepared to "break the ice" by sharing answers from your own life.

Step 2

If a lot of your group members come from troubled home situations, you might want to change the sample statements on the graffiti sheet to reflect their concerns. Here are some statements you might use:
- "I've never seen my father."
- "My mother is a crack addict."
- "Nobody's ever around when I get home from school."

Step 4

Add a third list to the board, under the heading "Code Red Eliminators." Explain that Code Red Eliminators are things that parents do that are illegal and/or massively destructive to the family bond. Among the Code Red Eliminators you might list are the following:
- *Sexual abuse (incest)*—Molestation or any sexual activity with a parent (or relative).
- *Physical abuse*—When discipline is no longer given to correct, but to hurt and harm.
- *Substance abuse*—A parent (or sibling) who has a drug or alcohol problem that will affect the family.
- *Verbal abuse*—When parents curse and yell at children and make no attempt to build a child's self-esteem.
- *Neglect*—When parents do not parent, but show no love or concern for their children.
- *Divorce*—Both parents can no longer get along and decide to end the marriage. Distribute paper and pencils. Separate group members so that they have room to write without anyone else reading their comments. Explain that you are going to begin an intervention policy for group members who have family problems and need your help—but that you need their suggestions as to how to go about it. After group members have written their suggestions, mention that if they need you to intercede for them in some fashion, they should write their initials in the upper corner of their papers. [NOTE: Don't do this activity unless you really plan to help.]

Step 1

Separate your junior highers and high schoolers into two teams. Give each team a set of "parent trait" cards from Repro Resource 1 and a pencil. Instruct the members of each team to work together in ranking the parent traits according to how important they think each one is. (There are a couple of blank cards provided, in case team members think of some additional traits.) Give the teams a few minutes to work. Then have each team share its list. Note the differences between the junior high team's list and the high school team's list. For those traits that are in significantly different positions on the two lists, ask each team to explain its reasoning in ranking them as it did.

Step 4

Separate your junior highers and high schoolers into two teams. Distribute paper and pencils to the junior high team. Instruct your junior highers to come up with five difficult situations a parent might face with his or her kids. (Situations might include finding out your son is taking drugs, having to tell your daughter she's too young to date, making your kids keep their bedrooms clean, etc.) After the junior highers have come up with five scenarios, they should read the scenarios one at a time to the high school team. At least two high schoolers should respond to each scenario. In responding, a high schooler should explain how he or she would handle the situation if he or she were a parent and then explain how his or her parents would handle the situation. Use this activity to lead into a discussion of what group members would and wouldn't like to copy about their parents.

Step 2

Compared to junior highers, most sixth graders still have a relatively compatible relationship with their parents (although they may be well aware of the conflicts of others). As you distribute the index cards, ask your sixth graders to write a shorter list—perhaps their top *five* parent pains. If you don't think that would work with your group members, have them (as a group) come up with a list of the top five problems their older siblings or older friends have with their parents.

Step 3

As you discuss Matthew 7:1-5, ask your sixth graders to think of examples of things that could be planks and specks in their own lives and relationships. Ask: **How do you know about these negative areas of your lives? Who pointed them out to you? How did you feel when they were pointed out to you?**

Date Used:

Approx. Time

Step 1: Building the Perfect Parent _____
o Extra Action
o Small Group
o Large Group
o Heard It All Before
o Mostly Girls
o Mostly Guys
o Extra Fun
o Media
o Combined Junior High/High School
Things needed:

Step 2: Top Ten Parent Pains _____
o Extra Action
o Mostly Guys
o Extra Fun
o Media
o Short Meeting Time
o Urban
o Sixth Grade
Things needed:

Step 3: Family Log Jams _____
o Heard It All Before
o Little Bible Background
o Short Meeting Time
o Sixth Grade
Things needed:

Step 4: Parenting 101 _____
o Small Group
o Fellowship & Worship
o Mostly Girls
o Urban
o Combined Junior High/High School
Things needed:

Step 5: One Perfect Father _____
o Large Group
o Little Bible Background
o Fellowship & Worship
Things needed:

The Fifth Commandment

HONOR THY FATHER AND THY MOTHER

when you think they're right.

YOUR GOALS FOR THIS SESSION:

Choose one or more

☐ To help kids recognize that honoring our parents is a commandment from God—not an optional suggestion.

☐ To help kids understand that there are times when we must choose to honor our parents even when we think they're wrong.

☐ To help kids choose one way to show honor to a parent this week.

☐ Other _____
_____

Your Bible Base:

Exodus 20:12
Colossians 3:12-21
Philippians 2:1-4

STEP

1

"P" Is for Parent

(Needed: Seven large pieces of paper, marker, pencils, masking tape)

Before the session, you'll need to prepare seven large pieces of paper. Each piece of paper should have one of the letters of the word "P-A-R-E-N-T-S" written on it. Tape the signs on a wall of your meeting area so that it's obvious to group members as they arrive that the signs spell out "parents."

To begin the session, distribute pencils to your group members and instruct them to write at least one word or phrase on each of the signs that starts with that letter and describes something about parents.

Encourage group members to write down as many words and phrases as they can think of. The more words you have to work with, the more effective the outcome of the activity will be. Point out that the words do not necessarily need to describe their own parents—just parents in general. Let group members have fun with the activity and don't be alarmed if it seems that they're venting some "bad attitudes."

After a few minutes, divide group members into seven teams. If necessary, a "team" can be made up of one person. Assign each team one of the signs on the wall. Instruct the teams to evaluate all the words and phrases on their signs in the following manner:

• They should *underline* all of the complimentary or positive words and phrases (e.g., "patient").

• They should *circle* all of the uncomplimentary or negative words and phrases (e.g., "pain in the neck").

• They should *ignore* all of the neutral words and phrases (e.g., "people").

Give the teams a few minutes to work. When they're finished, ask each team to give a total count for each category. Chances are pretty good that you'll have a majority of negative words and phrases. Take a minute or two to review some of the words and phrases that were given.

Ask: **Why do you suppose there are so many negative words and phrases on these sheets? Are things really that bad at home?** Allow time for a couple of group members to respond.

Then say: **As unpopular as it may sound, today we're going to talk about what it means to honor our parents.**

[NOTE: If, in the previous activity, the positive comments outnumbered the negative ones, you might want to check the Kool-Aid to see if it had too much sugar. If not, congratulate your group members on their mature insights. Then continue with the rest of the session. There's still plenty your group members can learn from this study.]

Pressure Pounds

(Needed: Paper, pencils)

Ask: **What do you suppose it feels like to be a parent?** (Some group members may say it probably feels good not having anybody tell you what to do. Others may say it probably feels good to be able to boss around your kids. Still others may say that being a parent is tough because of the pressure of being responsible for your kids.)

Say: **I'm sure you've heard your mom or dad say it a thousand times, but the truth is that being a parent isn't easy. A lot of the responsibilities your mom or dad live with must feel like weights they carry around with them all day. Let's take a look at some of the loads parents carry and see how yours are doing.**

The purpose of this activity is to give group members an understanding of the wide range of everyday things that can put pressure on parents. Perhaps it might also help group members develop an appreciation for what their parents go through as parents.

Give each group member a piece of paper and a pencil to calculate the "responsibility load" of one of their parents. Instruct group members to think of the parent they have the most difficulty getting along with. Then, as you read the following list, have them add up the "pressure pounds" their parents are experiencing.

• **For each kid in your family, add 10 pounds.**
• **For each kid that is a teenager or preschooler, add 5 pounds.**
• **If your parent is working at a new job—let's say less than a year—add 15 pounds.**
• **If your parent is unemployed** (this doesn't count homemakers), **add 25 pounds.**
• **If your parent recently had a loved one die, add 10 pounds.**
• **If your parent is divorced, separated, or widowed, add 50 pounds.**

• **If your parent's favorite team is on a losing streak, add 1 pound.**

• **If your parent travels a lot, add 10 pounds.**

• **If both of your parents work, add 15 pounds.**

• **If your parent has an illness, disease, or disability, add 20 pounds.**

• **If your parent is going to school or taking classes, add 10 pounds.**

• **If your parent argues or fights a lot with his or her spouse, add 15 pounds.**

• **If your parent works a lot of overtime or weekends, add 10 pounds.**

• **If the TV remote control is lost or broken, add 1 pound.**

• **If your parent often talks about being "broke" or having financial problems, add 15 pounds.**

• **If your parent talks about starting to feel old, add 10 pounds.**

• **If your parent has no time for regular exercise, add 10 pounds.**

• **If there's a pet in your household, add 2 pounds.**

• **If your parent does more than one job at church, add 10 pounds.**

• **If there's tension between your parent and you or your siblings, add 5 pounds.**

• **If your parent does most of the housework, add 5 pounds.**

• **If your parent does most of the cooking, add 5 pounds.**

• **If your parent is paying for college tuition, add 5 pounds.**

Feel free to add a couple of your own statements to the list.

Afterward, have group members total up their parents' "pressure pounds." Point out: **Some of your parents are living with some awfully big loads to carry. We don't often think about the pressures parents face. But those pressures are real—and they can have a serious effect on parents' lives.**

Be careful not to allow this to degenerate into a contest to see whose parent is the most frazzled. The reality here is that the parent with the most "pressure pounds" is *not* the winner! Stress isn't something to celebrate. Be sensitive to group members who are acknowledging major stresses in their parents' lives. These stresses often affect the kids as well.

STEP
3

Yes, Your Honor

(Needed: Chalkboard and chalk or newsprint and marker)

Say: **When we look at all the pressures our parents live with each day, it's a little easier to understand why God makes such a big deal about honoring our parents. In a number of places in the Bible, God makes His thoughts on the subject perfectly clear.**

Have someone read aloud Exodus 20:12. Then ask: **What does it mean to honor someone?** (It means to give that person respect, to do things for him or her, to show the person that he or she is valuable, to recognize his or her accomplishments or the things he or she does well, to put his or her interests ahead of ours, etc.)

Say: **When you guys were a little younger, honoring your parents was probably pretty easy. Your refrigerator doors were probably full of little signs and pictures you made at school that told your mom how great she was or that told your dad how much you loved him.**

Why does it sometimes seem harder to honor our parents as we get older? (As we get older, we begin to recognize some of their faults. It's also easier for us to be honest about our feelings when we're older.)

Then say: **By the same token, as we get older, the things we do to show others that we value and honor them are more mature and perhaps more meaningful.**

What are some things you can do to honor your parents now that you couldn't do when you were six or seven? (Talk to them about things that matter; get their advice on tough decisions you have to make; compliment them on things they do well; understand some of their pressures and encourage them or pray for them; etc.)

Say: **We'll come back to some of these practical ideas for honoring your mom or dad in a minute. But I thought you might be interested in knowing that honoring each other is a rule for the whole family, and not just kids. Turn in your Bibles to Colossians 3.**

Have someone read aloud verses 18-21. Then ask: **How can a wife honor her husband?** (By supporting his decisions, encouraging him, respecting his opinions, praising him, etc.) Try to avoid a long discussion on the true definition of "submission" here. But at least point out that

OPTIONS

EXTRA ACTION

HEARD IT ALL BEFORE

LITTLE BIBLE BACKGROUND

MOSTLY GIRLS

MOSTLY GUYS

MEDIA

URBAN

submission doesn't mean being a "doormat" to be walked on.

How can a husband show honor to his wife? (By providing for her, encouraging her, respecting her opinions, praising her, etc.)

Say: **We've already talked about how kids need to honor their parents. But take a look at the last verse in the passage that was just read. How does a parent honor his or her children?** (By not embittering or discouraging them.)

Talk briefly about what it means to embitter or exasperate someone. Ask group members to name some things kids experience at home that are discouraging.

Say: **OK, so we all have a responsibility to honor one another. But how do we do that? In the verses just before the ones we read are some specific instructions for husbands, wives, parents, and even kids on how to honor one another. Let's take a look.**

Have someone read aloud Colossians 3:12-17. As the person reads, have the rest of the group members call out words in the passage that describe how we should treat our family members. Write the words on the board as they're named. Your list should include the following words: compassion, kindness, humility, gentleness, patience, forgive, love, peace, and thankful.

Ask: **If you and your family used these kinds of attitudes toward each other, what differences would it make in your family?** Get responses from as many group members as possible.

Then say: **Let's wrap up our discussion by looking at a passage from a letter Paul wrote to his friends in the city of Philippi. The passage is found in Philippians 2.**

Have someone read aloud verses 2-5. Comment briefly on the fact that these are the attitudes Jesus had and asks us to follow.

STEP

4

Putting It into Practice

(Needed: Seven signs from Step 1, marker, pencils, masking tape)

Say: **We've seen that honoring members of our families—especially our parents—is something God commands us to do. So, now what? What do we do with this information? Let's try another exercise with the letter signs we used earlier.**

Turn over the seven signs you used in Step 1. As before, write one of the letters of the word "P-A-R-E-N-T-S" on each sign. Then instruct group members to write on the signs ideas for how they could show honor to their parents. (Ideally, the ideas should start with the seven letters on the signs; but, be flexible.)

Give group members a few minutes to work. When they're finished, read aloud their suggestions. Use the following ideas to supplement group members' responses.

P—Pick up after myself when I make a mess; pray for my parents.

A—Ask for permission before I do something; always call if I'm going to get in later than I'm supposed to.

R—Respect my parents' privacy; return things to where I found them.

E—Explain to my parents how much they mean to me; extend courtesy and politeness to them.

N—Never talk negatively about my parents to my friends; notice when my parents do something nice for me and thank them for it.

T—Talk to my parents nicely, rather than whining or yelling at them; take out the garbage, without having to be told to.

S—Say "I love you" more often; send flowers to my mom for no special reason.

This part of the exercise probably will be tougher for your group members than the first part (in Step 1) was. Be prepared to help them get started, but make sure to leave a lot of room for them to come up with their own suggestions. Those are the ideas they'll feel some ownership of.

Briefly review the list with your group members. Comment on a few of the suggestions to help group members understand that honoring parents involves more than just how we feel about them—it means putting some things into action so parents actually feel honored.

O P T I O N S

HEARD IT ALL BEFORE

LITTLE BIBLE BACKGROUND

MEDIA

SHORT MEETING TIME

JR. HIGH HIGH SCHOOL COMBINED

SIXTH GRADE

STEP
5

MVP——My Valuable Parent

(Needed: Paper, pencils, copies of Repro Resource 3, markers)

Distribute paper and pencils. Then say: **Let's think of some practical ways we can start to honor our parents this week. Choose one action from the lists we've made on these sheets to work on this week. Try to choose an action that doesn't come naturally to you—one that would really show your**

parents that you're making an effort to honor them. Write the action on your piece of paper. Then make a commitment to follow through on that action throughout the week. Keep your piece of paper handy throughout the week as a reminder of your commitment.

Distribute copies of "MVP Award" (Repro Resource 3) and markers. Explain to your group members that this award will serve as kind of a "primer" for their parents, to let them know that their kids are thinking about them and are taking specific actions to honor them. (Without this "primer," parents may be suspicious of their kids' motives—or they may faint dead away when their kids try to show them honor!)

Give group members a few minutes to work on their awards. They should write in their parents' names, as well as what their parents are being honored for ("For driving me to and from soccer practice every day and for never missing a game"). If there's time, group members might also decorate their awards accordingly.

Encourage group members to leave their awards in places where their parents will find them, rather than making a big deal out of the presentations.

Close the session in prayer, asking God to help your group members follow through on their commitments to honor their parents.

THE "MOST VALUABLE PARENT(S)" TITLE

is awarded to

_____

This award is given in appreciation for

_____

_____

_____

_____

_____

Step 2

For this activity you'll need several cardboard boxes and large, heavy books. Have group members form pairs. Give each pair a cardboard box. (If possible, make sure all of the boxes are approximately the same size.) One at a time, have each pair bring its cardboard box to the front of the room, turn it upside down, and begin stacking books on top of it. The pair that stacks the most books on its box before the box collapses is the winner. Afterward, draw an analogy between the weight that was supported by the boxes and the "pressure pounds" that weigh on parents.

Step 3

Have group members form pairs. Instruct each pair to come up with a brief roleplay demonstrating what might happen if a teenager tried to communicate with his or her parents in the same way he or she communicated with them when he or she was a kid (six or seven years old). For instance, one pair might have the teenager throwing a tantrum if he or she doesn't get his or her way. Another pair might have the teenager whining and talking like a baby. Another pair might have the teenager pouting after being reprimanded. Another pair might have the teenager clinging to his or her parent when he or she is being dropped off at school. One person in each pair will play the teenager; the other person will play the parent. Give the pairs a few minutes to prepare; then have them present their roleplays. Afterward, point out that we have the opportunity to communicate with our parents on a more adult level now. We also have the opportunities to honor them in ways we couldn't when we were six or seven.

Step 1

Rather than having group members form teams to evaluate the words and phrases on the "P-A-R-E-N-T-S" sheet, evaluate them as a group. You will read each word or phrase aloud. If group members think it's complimentary, they should stand; if they think it's negative, they should sit on the floor; if they think it's neutral, they should squat—halfway between standing and sitting. Keep tally on the board of how many words or phrases are positive, how many are negative, and how many are neutral.

Step 5

Take advantage of the size of your group by giving group members an opportunity to respond personally to each other's ideas. After each person chooses an action to honor his or her parents, have him or her share the idea with the rest of the group. Then have each of the rest of the group members offer a comment or piece of advice to the person concerning his or her idea. For instance, let's say someone chose "Explain to my parents how much they mean to me" as his or her action. One of the other group members might say, "Make sure not to give them the impression that you're being nice to them because you want something from them." Someone else might say, "Don't go overboard with your comments—just be honest." Someone else might say, "I tried that with my parents and this is what happened ..."

Step 1

With a large group, you'll want to avoid having all of your group members crowded around the sheets at the same time trying to write. Instead, explain the activity while your group members are still in their seats and give them a few minutes to brainstorm what they'll write. Then have them line up single-file next to the first sheet. Give each person approximately 15 seconds to write his or her ideas on each sheet. After about 15 seconds he or she will move on to the next sheet. If you keep the line moving, you should be able to finish the activity in 5-10 minutes.

Step 2

As you read the list, write each item on the board. Then, after group members have totaled up their parents' "pressure pounds," have them form groups of four. In their groups they should discuss the following questions:

• Which of these items on the board would you say is most stressful for your parent?
• Which of these items is most stressful for you?
• Which of these items is hardest for you to understand? In other words, which do you think shouldn't bother your parent as much as it does?
• Which of these items could you do something about?

Step 3

Many churches tend to emphasize passages like Ephesians 6:1-3 and Colossians 3:20, which focus on children's responsibility to honor and obey their parents. Many churches also tend to downplay passages like Ephesians 6:4 and Colossians 3:21, which focus on parents' responsibility to their kids. So it might be an interesting change of pace for your group members to focus on Ephesians 6:4 and Colossians 3:21. Ask the following questions:

• **Do your parents ever "exasperate" you? If so, how do they do it?**
• **Do your parents ever make you feel bitter or discouraged? If so, how do they do it?**
• **How does the way your parents treat you affect the way you treat them?**
• **How do you wish your parents would treat you?**
• **How could you let your parents know how you feel?**

Step 4

Because so little information is given about Jesus' youth, your group members who've "heard it all before" may think of Jesus only as a baby or as a man. Focus group members' attention on one of the rare Bible passages that talks about Jesus' childhood: Luke 2:41-52. Say: **It seems like Jesus may not have honored His parents in this passage. After all, they were worried because they couldn't find Him. And when they did find Him, He talked about having to be in His "Father's house." What do you think of His actions?** If no one mentions it, point out that God was Jesus' Father, and took priority in Jesus' life. Jesus wasn't being disrespectful to Mary and Joseph. He was just informing them of His priorities. Note that verse 51 says, "Then [Jesus] went down to Nazareth with [Mary and Joseph] and was obedient to them." This is the example of Jesus that we are to follow.

Step 3

Some of your group members who aren't familiar with the commands of Scripture may reason, "Since my parents don't obey the command not to discourage or exasperate their kids, I don't have to obey the command to honor them." Point out that Colossians 3:21 and Exodus 20:12 are not "If ... then" statements. We do not honor our parents only if they hold up their end of the bargain first. We have to honor them, no matter what. Encourage several group members to offer their opinions of this "honor no matter what" situation.

Step 4

If your group members come from non-Christian households, they may be experiencing more severe parent problems than their peers who come from Christian households. Help group members see that the Bible covers all kinds of parent conflicts—Jacob deceiving and lying to his father Isaac (Genesis 27), Saul throwing a spear in anger at his son Jonathan (I Samuel 20), and the prodigal son taking his inheritance and leaving home (Luke 15), to name a few. Suggest that the fact that so many "modern-day" kinds of situations are covered in the Bible makes Scripture relevant for parent-teen relationships today.

Step 2

Have someone read aloud Matthew 11:28. ("Come to me, all you who are weary and burdened, and I will give you rest.") Then, as a group, brainstorm a list of ways God can remove burdens from our parents' lives and give them rest. Write group members' suggestions on the board as they are named. If no one mentions it, suggest that one of the ways to remove burdens from parents' lives is to have their children honor and obey them. Point out to your group members that *they* could be part of God's plan in bringing rest to their parents. Have a moment of silent prayer, thanking God for caring enough about us to give us rest when we're "weary and burdened."

Step 5

Have group members pair up with someone they know fairly well. If not all of your group members know someone well in your group, have the partners take a few minutes to share some things about their parents with each other. Afterward each person should name one thing about his or her partner's parents that sounds good. (For instance, someone might say, "It's really cool that you and your dad both like baseball. I have a hard time getting my dad to watch a game with me.") Hearing their peers say good things about their parents may help your group members begin to see their parents in a different light.

Step 3

Distribute paper and pencils. While you read aloud Colossians 3:12-17, each girl should make her own list of the words in the passage that describe how we should treat our family members. After you read aloud Philippians 2:2-5, group members should add at least one item or phrase from that passage to their lists.

Step 5

Have your group members review the ideas they wrote on the "P-A-R-E-N-T-S" signs in Step 4. Instruct them to find any ideas that could be adapted as a group activity. Have your group members brainstorm together ways they can honor the parents of all the girls in the group. For instance, your group members might write a "round-robin" letter of appreciation or they might prepare and serve (or deliver) meals for the parents. When your group members have decided on a way to honor the parents as a group, help them do the planning to put their idea into action.

Step 2

If some of your guys are into weightlifting, they may be more attuned to the "pressure pounds" analogy. Ask: **How much weight can you benchpress? How much can you squat? How much can you deadlift?** After you've gone through the "pressure pounds" list, ask: **How much weight do you think you could carry around all day?** Get responses from as many group members as possible. Then ask: **What kinds of effects do you think these "pressure pounds" have on parents who have to "carry them around" all day?** Encourage several group members to respond.

Step 3

After you discuss Exodus 20:12, use the following questions to guide your discussion. (Be sensitive to kids whose parents are divorced, widowed, or unmarried as you discuss these questions.)
• **Is it easier for you to honor your mother or your father? Why?**
• **Is it easier for you to honor your parents verbally—by what you say—or physically—by what you do?**
• **Do your friends ever pressure you not to honor your parents? If so, how do they do that?**
• **Do you feel like your parents honor you? Do they treat you like a man or like a little kid? Explain.**
• **How does the way your parents treat you affect the way you treat them?**

Step 1

Say: **Science and technology have perfected many procedures, industries, and gadgets. So what if they turned their attention to creating the perfect robotic parents? What would be the result? What kind of design and features would these parents have?** Have group members form teams of two or three. Distribute large sheets of paper, pencils, and markers to each team. Instruct the teams to come up with designs for the perfect robotic parents. For instance, the perfect robotic father might have a specially designed arm to throw footballs with perfect spirals and baseballs with incredible curves. He might also have an automatic teller machine on his hip to dispense money whenever his kids need it. The perfect robotic mother might have eyes all around her head so she can see everything her kids do. She might also have vacuums on the bottom of her feet so she can clean the floor while walking. When the teams are finished, have them explain their creations. Then point out that because our parents *aren't* perfect, we sometimes have trouble honoring them.

Step 2

Ask for a couple volunteers to participate in a contest of strength and speed. Explain that the contestants will be competing to see who can pull people on a sheet of plastic from one part of the room to another in the shortest amount of time. Choose one member of the group to be pulled on the plastic for the first round. Time each contestant and write his or her results on the board. For the second round, add another person on the plastic to be pulled. Compare group members' times from the first round to the second round. Continue adding another person each round until your contestants are unable to pull. Then discuss how carrying around a lot of "pressure pounds" can affect a parent's "performance."

Step 3

Record clips from several TV sitcoms featuring families. Among the shows you might record are reruns of *The Brady Bunch, Leave It to Beaver, My Three Sons, The Cosby Show, Roseanne, Home Improvement, Family Matters,* and *The Simpsons.* Try to record scenes that show kids interacting with their parents. Play back the clips for your group members and discuss which ones show kids honoring their parents and which ones show kids dishonoring their parents. Then discuss whether the media has any influence on the way we act toward our parents.

Step 4

Bring in a video camera or tape recorder. Have your group members think of an everyday, normal thing they might say to their parents. (For instance, "Where's my sweater?") Record each group member saying his or her statement three different ways. First, he or she should say it happily or cheerfully. Second, he or she should say it angrily. Third, he or she should say it whiningly. Play back the recording for your group and point out that *how* we say something is as important as *what* we say.

Step 1

Rather than taking the time to have group members come up to the signs and write, play a quick game. Have group members sit in a circle. You will give them a letter, and they will have to come up with a word or phrase (beginning with that letter) that describes something about parents. Group members will have five seconds to come up with a word or phrase. If a person fails to do so, he or she is out. Once everyone has had a turn, call out another letter, and repeat the process. (The letters you will use are P, A, R, E, N, T, S.) Continue the game until only one person remains. Afterward, discuss how many of the words and phrases named were positive, how many were negative, and how many were neutral.

Step 4

If you didn't use the signs in Step 1, you'll need to make some adjustments in this step. Write the letters P, A, R, E, N, T, S on small slips of paper and put them in a container. Have group members draw a slip of paper and then come up with an idea—that begins with the letter they drew—of how to show honor to their parents. Give group members a few minutes to work; then have everyone share his or her response with the rest of the group. Write the responses on the board as they are named. Then have group members choose one idea from the board to work on with their parents.

Step 2

Here are some additional "pressure pound" scenarios that may be reality for urban parents:

- **For each child selling or using drugs, add 20 pounds.**
- **If your parents are worried about your safety in the community, add 15 pounds.**
- **If any of your immediate family members** (brother, sister, parent) **were killed by gunfire or died unsuspectingly in the last year, add 40 pounds.**
- **If your parents have an unmarried daughter who is pregnant or an unmarried son who is a father, add 10 pounds.**
- **If your parents have a child who is a homosexual, add 10 pounds.**

Step 3

Some of your group members may have grown up in single-parent homes. One of their parents may have died when the child was young or ran from parental responsibility. As a result, some of your group members may not even know one of their parents. If that's the case with your group, have your young people brainstorm together ways to honor a parent they've never known. After considering some things that could be done, let them decide what they can do to improve their understanding and/or relationship with this missing parent. Help group members recognize that knowledge about a missing parent can lead to a better understanding of themselves.

JR.HIGH / HIGH SCHOOL COMBINED

SIXTH GRADE

PLANNING CHECKLIST

JR. HIGH/HIGH SCHOOL COMBINED

Step 4

To make the "P-A-R-E-N-T-S" activity a little more focused, separate your junior highers and high schoolers into two groups. Instruct your junior highers to focus on activities that have to do with curfew and jobs around the house. In other words, how can they honor their parents through their curfew and chores? (As much as possible, their suggestions should start with P, A, R, E, N, T, and S.) Use the following suggestions to supplement your junior highers' ideas: "Pick up the empty chip bags and soda cans when I finish eating in front of the TV"; "Always call home if I'm going to be late"; etc. Instruct your high schoolers to focus on activities that have to do with driving and friends. In other words, how can they honor their parents through their use of the car and by the company they keep? Use the following suggestions to supplement your high schoolers' ideas: "Put gas in the car when I'm finished with it"; "Turn around and walk out if I discover that people are drinking or taking drugs at a party I'm attending"; etc.

Step 5

After your junior highers have chosen an action with which to show honor to their parents, have them share their ideas with the group. Then encourage your high schoolers to respond to those ideas— perhaps giving advice on what to do and what not to do in implementing the strategy, or relating experiences of when they tried similar actions with their parents. High schoolers should respond in a spirit of helpfulness; they should not belittle or make fun of your junior highers' ideas. The idea is to develop a "mentoring" relationship between your high schoolers and your junior highers.

SIXTH GRADE

Step 2

Your sixth graders may not have a complete sense of the responsibility load of their parents—especially when it comes to the stresses of their parents' careers. So instead of going through the entire list of "pressure pound" scenarios with your group members, choose ten or so scenarios from the list that you think would be the most relevant (and recognizable) to them.

Step 4

To stimulate your group members' thinking, brainstorm as a group a few general ways to show honor to parents. Then have your kids form seven teams. Assign each team one of the "P-A-R-E-N-T-S" signs. Instruct each team to come up with at least two ideas for honoring parents that begin with its assigned letter. If you don't have enough kids for seven teams, give two or more letters to each team.

Give the teams a few minutes to work; then have them share their ideas. After each team has shared, ask for additional ideas from the rest of the group.

PLANNING CHECKLIST

Date Used:

Approx. Time

Step 1: "P" Is for Parents _____
o Small Group
o Large Group
o Extra Fun
o Short Meeting Time
Things needed:

Step 2: Pressure Pounds _____
o Extra Action
o Large Group
o Fellowship & Worship
o Mostly Guys
o Extra Fun
o Urban
o Sixth Grade
Things needed:

Step 3: Yes, Your Honor _____
o Extra Action
o Heard It All Before
o Little Bible Background
o Mostly Girls
o Mostly Guys
o Media
o Urban
Things needed:

Step 4: Putting It into Practice _____
o Heard It All Before
o Little Bible Background
o Media
o Short Meeting Time
o Combined Junior High/High School
o Sixth Grade
Things needed:

Step 5: MVP—My Valuable Parent _____
o Small Group
o Fellowship & Worship
o Mostly Girls
o Combined Junior High/High School
Things needed:

3 The Great Breakaway

YOUR GOALS FOR THIS SESSION:

C h o o s e   o n e   o r   m o r e

☐ To help kids recognize that they can help make their transition from childhood to adulthood easier by participating cooperatively in the process.

☐ To help kids understand that it's OK to want to establish an identity that is separate from their parents.

☐ To help kids decide to take on one specific responsibility in their families to indicate their willingness to act responsibly and earn a right of adulthood.

☐ Other _____

Your Bible Base:

Luke 15:11-20

Trading Places

(Needed: Two pieces of lumber)

Before the session, set out two 2" x 4" pieces of lumber. Each board should be between four and five feet long. Make sure there is enough room between the boards to let people move freely.

Ask for four volunteers—two pairs—to participate in a contest. Have the members of each pair stand on one of the boards, facing each other. The object of the game is for the members of each pair to change places on the board without falling off or touching the floor. The first pair to successfully change places wins.

To stir up your group members' imaginations and add some excitement and humor to the contest, you could have them pretend that the floor is shark-infested waters, an alligator pit, or a toxic-waste dump.

Give as many kids as possible a chance to compete, letting the winning pair stay on and having challengers try to outdo them. After all the challenges have been made, declare a winner.

Then ask: **What was the secret of success in this activity?** (Helping each other, cooperating, talking to each other, going slowly, etc.)

Say: **You guys are at a time in your lives where your position in the family is about to start changing. You're moving toward being an adult with all the rights, privileges, and responsibilities that come with growing up. It's a big change—and an important one. One of the things that needs to happen as you become an adult is that your relationship with your parents has to change. It's sort of like what you saw happening on the boards a few minutes ago.**

Point out that, like changing positions on the board, changing your relationship with your parents involves helping one another, talking to one another, cooperating with each other, and going slowly.

Growing Up in a Hurry

(Needed: Copies of Repro Resource 4, pencils)

Ask: **How many of you have ever wished you were grown up—that one day you would just suddenly become an adult and never be treated like a kid again?** Probably most of your group members have wished this at one time or another. Ask a couple of volunteers to explain their reasons for wanting to be an adult.

Distribute copies of "The Adventures of the Suddenly Grown Up" (Repro Resource 4) and pencils. Give group members a few minutes to read the story.

Then say: **Think about what Stan's life will be like now that he's grown up. What kinds of things will he be able to do now that he wasn't able to do before? What kinds of problems will he face now that he didn't have to face before?**

Have group members write or draw their ideas at the bottom of the sheet. Give them a few minutes to work; then have them share their responses with the rest of the group.

Group members might mention that, for Stan, growing up would mean being able to drive, being able to move out of his parents' house, being able to earn a lot of money, etc. They also might mention that growing up would mean more responsibility, having to get a job, having to pay bills, having to act "mature," etc.

Point out that becoming an adult is a process; it's a transition that takes time—perhaps as long as five or six years. It takes so much time because there's a lot of preparation that needs to be done. There are things we need to know, situations we have to experience, and wisdom we have to gain before we're ready for adulthood.

The Prodigal

Say: **Jesus tells a story of a young man who decided to grow up very quickly. In the process, the young man made a lot of really dumb moves—and a couple of pretty smart moves. Jesus' story is found in Luke 15. I'll summarize it for you.**

Listen carefully as I read. Whenever you hear someone in the story making a bad move, shout "bad move" as loudly as you can. Whenever you hear someone in the story making a good move, shout out "good move."

A man had two sons (good move). **One day the younger son said to his father, "I want my share of your estate now instead of when you die"** (bad move). **His father agreed to divide his wealth between his sons** (bad move). **A few days later, the younger son packed all of his belongings and took a trip to a distant land** (bad move). **There he wasted all of his money on parties and prostitutes** (bad move).

About the time his money was gone, a great famine swept over all the land, and the younger son began to starve (bad move). **He persuaded a local farmer to hire him to feed his pigs** (good move). **The boy became so hungry that even the pods he was feeding the swine looked good to him. No one gave him anything.**

When he finally came to his senses (good move), **he said to himself, "At home, even the hired men have more than enough food to eat, and here I am dying of hunger! I will go home** (good move) **to my father and say, 'Father I have sinned against both heaven and you and I am no longer worthy to be called your son. Please take me on as a hired man'** (good move)**." So he returned home to his father** (good move). **While he was still a long distance away, his father saw him coming and was filled with loving pity** (good move). **The father ran and embraced his son and kissed him** (good move).

Have group members form teams of three or four. Distribute paper and pencils to each team. Instruct the teams to turn in their Bibles to the story you just summarized from Luke 15:11-20. Have them re-read the story. Every time they identify a "bad move" on the part of the younger son, they should write down a better choice he could have made. (For instance, rather than squandering his money on parties and prostitutes, he could have invested it, bought his own house with it, used it to start a business, etc.) Then the teams should describe how the Luke 15 story might have ended differently if the younger son had made better choices.

Give the teams a few minutes to work. When everyone is finished, have each team share its ideas.

STEP
4

Grown-Up Concentration

(Needed: Copies of Repro Resource 5, copies of Repro Resource 6)

Before the session, you'll need to cut apart copies of "Concentration Cards" (Repro Resource 5). You'll then need to attach those cards to copies of "Concentration" (Repro Resource 6). To do this, cut out the slots (indicated by dotted lines) on Repro Resource 6 and slide the "concentration cards" facedown into the slots to cover the rebus on Repro Resource 6.

Have group members form pairs. Distribute a covered copy of Repro Resource 6 to each pair. Explain that the facedown slips of paper are "privilege and responsibility" cards. These cards list a variety of benefits of growing up, as well as some responsibilities that come with being an adult. Point out that each privilege card has a corresponding responsibility card. For example, one privilege of growing up is having a driver's license and driving a car. The corresponding responsibility is to know and follow the rules of the road.

Explain that the members of each pair will be finding and matching these cards in a contest similar to the game "Concentration."

Players will take turns turning over two cards at a time. If a player finds a matching "privilege and responsibility" pair, he or she gets to remove those two cards and guess the rebus message underneath. If the player does not find a matching pair, he or she turns the cards back over and forfeits his or her turn. [NOTE: For easier identification, the privilege and responsibility cards are numbered. All group members have to do is match numbers on the cards.]

As the matching pairs are found, more and more of the rebus will be visible, making it easier for players to guess the message. The rebus message is "I'm not a kid anymore."

After all of the pairs have finished the exercise, say: **For every privilege associated with being an adult, there are some**

tough responsibilities that go along with it. Growing up is a wonderful, exciting experience—but it also involves taking responsibility for our choices and earning the right to have the benefits or privileges that we look forward to.

STEP
5

Shock Their Socks Off!

Say: **Think of a responsibility you could take this week to show your parents that you're really serious about growing up. What could you do in your home or family that your parents wouldn't expect you to do in their wildest dreams—something so mature and grown up that it would shock their socks off?**

Find a partner—perhaps the person you played "Concentration" with earlier. Tell your partner what it is you plan to do this week to show your family that you really are serious about growing up. Then, if possible, check on your partner once or twice during the week to see how well he or she is doing.

Give the partners a minute or two to think of some ideas. If time permits, ask a couple of volunteers to share their ideas.

Point out to your group members that the surprise of their actions might be so great for their parents that their parents won't know how to respond right away. Emphasize that the real joy in this exercise is knowing that they are doing the mature thing, not that they are able to manipulate their parents into some new form of submission.

Close the session in prayer, asking God to help your group members in their continuing process of becoming a grown-up.

The Adventures of the
SUDDENLY GROWN UP

Stan's fourteenth birthday party was OK–but it wasn't exactly what he wanted. There was plenty of cake and ice cream, and all his friends and family were there. But Stan wanted more.

When Paul, Stan's brother, turned seventeen, he and his friends were allowed to go to the drive-in (for a double feature)–and then, *afterward,* they went bowling for a couple hours. Paul didn't get in until *after 3:00 in the morning!*

Stan wanted to do the same kind of thing for his birthday. But his parents wouldn't let him. They said he was still too young to be staying out that late. Instead, Stan was allowed to rent a couple videos and have three of his friends stay overnight. Big deal.

When it came time for Stan to blow out the candles on his birthday cake and make a wish, he knew exactly what he'd wish for.

I wish I were a grown-up, Stan thought to himself as he blew out the candles. Ten seconds later, as his friends and family looked on in amazement, Stan's wish came true. He suddenly became a grown-up.

Concentration Cards

1

As an adult, I have the privilege of having a driver's license and driving a car.

1

As an adult, I am responsible to know the rules of the road and live by them.

2

As an adult, I have the privilege of deciding what I want to eat and when to eat it.

2

As an adult, I have the responsibility of my health, and perhaps my family's.

3

As an adult, I have the privilege of deciding what to watch on TV and which movies to see.

3

As an adult, I am responsible to choose carefully the kinds of media messages I allow into my mind.

4

As an adult, I have the privilege of choosing what time I go to bed and how late I sleep.

4

As an adult, I am responsible to make good decisions about how I use my time.

5

As an adult, I have the privilege of picking my own friends and choosing whom to hang around with.

5

As an adult, I am responsible to know that the friends I pick will affect my life.

6

As an adult, I have the privilege of making my own decisions about drugs and alcohol.

6

As an adult, I am responsible for the harm I do myself or others while drinking or on drugs.

7

As an adult in college, I have the privilege of deciding whether or not to go to class.

7

As an adult in college, I am responsible for my grades and the money I spend on my classes.

8

As an adult, I have the privilege of earning as much money as I can.

8

As an adult, I am responsible to use my money wisely for bills, tithes, living expenses, etc.

Concentration

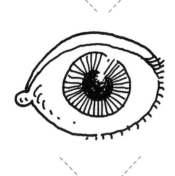 **+M**

A

A+ 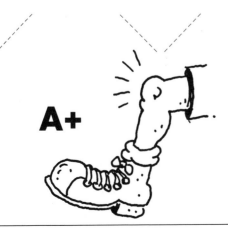 **M+**

Step 1

Rather than having group members trade places on the boards, try a more active approach. Ask for three volunteers at a time to participate in a race. Two of the volunteers will be working as a team; the other will be working solo. Set down two sheets of newspaper. Explain that your contestants will be competing to see who can get from one end of the room to the other first—on the newspaper—without touching the floor or tearing the paper. The solo person probably will have to shuffle, scoot, and gyrate to move. The two contestants who are working together should decide which one will stand on the paper. That person may not touch the floor at all. However, his or her partner may. These two may move by having the person on the paper jump forward while his or her partner pulls the newspaper under him or her. If the two establish a regular pace, they should have an advantage over the person working solo.

Afterward, draw an analogy to the process of becoming an adult: It's easier when you work in cooperation with your parents, rather than trying to do it alone.

Step 3

Ask for two volunteers to roleplay the story of the prodigal son while you read it. Assign one person to be the son and the other to be the father. The actors will speak and act according to what you read. You can have some fun with the fact that your actors won't know what they're supposed to do next (especially when you read, "He ran to his son, threw his arms around him and kissed him").

Rather than having group members form teams to discuss the story, replay the roleplay again. This time, however, when group members call out "bad move," the actors should freeze. Group members will then call out suggestions for better choices the characters could make. The actors must then say and do what the other group members suggest.

Step 1

Have your group members line up single-file. If possible, put the two smallest people in the group at each end of the line. Each should be standing on a newspaper or some other object so that he or she is not "directly" touching the floor. Explain that the two people at the end of the line must trade places—without touching the floor at all and without moving the newspaper or object they're standing on. Group members will work together in accomplishing this goal. However, the other group members may not move from their single-file positions.

There are several ways to do this. The other group members may get down on all fours (remaining in their single-file positions) and allow the two end people to walk across them. The other group members may pick up the end people and "pass" them across. Or the people on the end could "jump" across, landing on the other group members' feet so that they don't touch the ground.

Afterward, discuss how the cooperation involved in the activity is similar to the cooperation needed between parents and kids as the kids become adults.

Step 4

Rather than having kids pair up to play the "Concentration" game, play it as a group. However, you may want to "raise the stakes" a little. Each time a group member fails to match two cards, have him or her perform some kind of stunt in front of the group. Here are some ideas for stunts you might use:
• Do ten pushups while reciting the alphabet backwards.
• Whistle the theme to *Gilligan's Island* while standing on one leg.
• Lead the group in a cheer.
• Run around the room backward while you call out the names of everyone in the group.
• Tell your favorite (clean) joke in front of the group.

Step 1

Have group members form teams of five. If possible, make sure that all teams have both big, strong people and small, lightweight people on them. Set up an obstacle course or racetrack in your meeting area. Explain that the teams will be competing to see which team can finish the course first—while carrying one of its members. Have each team choose one member (probably the smallest person on the team) to carry. The other teammates may hold the person over their heads, on their shoulders, by his or her arms and legs, or any other way they want. The only stipulation is that the person being carried may not touch the ground.

Have the teams line up behind a start/finish line. When you say go, they will run around the course as quickly as possible. If a team allows the person being carried to touch the floor at all, it must start over. Obviously, the more teams you have, the crazier the competition will be.

Afterward, point out that successfully navigating the course required cooperation among the team members. In the same way, successfully navigating the transition between childhood and adulthood requires cooperation between parents and kids.

Step 3

To get group members more personally involved in this study, have them form teams of four. Distribute index cards and pencils to each team. Instruct each team to read Luke 15:11-20 and come up with a list of the top four "bad moves" made by the younger son in the story. Then have the teams list four better choices the younger son could have made, and describe how the story might have turned out differently if he'd made the better choices. Give the teams a few minutes to work. When they're finished, have each one share its responses with the rest of the group.

HEARD IT ALL BEFORE

LITTLE BIBLE BACKGROUND

FELLOWSHIP & WORSHIP

Step 3

If your group members are overly familiar with the story of the prodigal son, use the story of Jacob and Isaac in Genesis 27 as your Bible study text. Have volunteers take turns reading aloud verses 1-41. Then, as a group, list the "bad moves" Jacob made in obtaining the blessing from his father. Afterward, go back through the story and have group members offer suggestions for better choices Jacob could have made to get Isaac's blessing—and how the story might have turned out differently if Jacob had made those better choices.

Ask: **How do kids today deceive their parents to get what they want? How might these deceptions affect a person's relationship with his or her parents?**

Step 5

Kids who've "heard it all before" may be able to recite from memory several *general* things they can do for their parents—"help out around the house," "tell my parents how much I appreciate them," "honor and obey my parents," etc.

To get beyond this nonspecific attitude, list on the board several specific things kids can do to demonstrate maturity to their parents. Have group members explain which ideas would and which ideas wouldn't work with their parents and why. Here are some ideas you might use:
• Offering to babysit your little brother or sister on Friday night rather than going out with your friends so your parents can have some "away" time alone.
• Buying your mother a "thank you" card in which you list twenty-five things you're thankful for about her.
• Refusing to argue, complain, or question the next time your parents tell you you can't do something you really want to do.
• Treating your whole family to ice cream with your allowance money.
• Giving up an entire Saturday to clean the house and work in the yard—without being asked to.

Step 3

If your group members are unfamiliar with the story of the prodigal son, you may want to give them a more complete understanding of its meaning and significance. You might say something like: **Not only does this story teach us some valuable lessons about making good decisions, it also gives us an idea of how God feels about us. The father in the story represents God; the younger son represents sinners. How do you think the father felt when his son decided to leave? How do you think God feels when He sees people sinning?** (Sad.)

Why didn't the father prevent his son from leaving? Why doesn't God prevent us from sinning? (We have free will; we are given the chance to choose to do right.)

How did the father react when the son repented and came home? How does God react when people ask for forgiveness from Him? (He welcomes us with open arms.)

Step 5

You might want to wrap up the session by explaining the biblical principle of "reaping what you sow." Have volunteers read aloud Job 4:8 and Galatians 6:7. Ask: **How would you reword this principle in easier-to-understand terms?** ("What you dish out, you will get back." "If you act like a jerk, people will treat you like a jerk.")

How does this principle apply to the topic of our session—growing up? (If you act like a mature person around your parents, they will treat you like a mature person. If you act childishly, they will treat you like a child.)

If you have time, distribute index cards and pencils. Instruct group members to write out the text of Job 4:8 or Galatians 6:7 on their cards. Encourage them to keep the cards handy as reminders of the "reap what you sow" principle.

Step 4

After the partners have completed the "Concentration" game, have them briefly share with each other an example of a setback they've had in demonstrating their maturity to their parents. After each person has shared, his or her partner should offer words of encouragement and/ or advice.

For instance, let's say one partner shares the following setback: "I threw a fit when my parents told me I couldn't go to the mall with my friends. I yelled and screamed and called them names. They said I was acting like a spoiled little kid. I think it'll take a long time before they think of me as being mature or grown up." His or her partner might offer the following words of advice: "If you apologize to them and let them know that *you* know how childish you were, they might respect your judgment and forget about the incident more easily."

Step 5

Wrap up the session with a praise activity. Write the words "Thank You, God" vertically in big letters on the board. Then, as a group, brainstorm some benefits of maturing/becoming an adult that begin with each of the letters of "Thank You, God." Write the benefits on the board next to the appropriate letters. (For instance, "T" might be "Talking on the phone with my friends as long as I want"; "H" might be "Having my own car"; etc.) When group members have named at least one benefit for each letter, have them form a circle for closing prayer. Instruct each person to choose one of the benefits on the board and say a sentence prayer, thanking God for it.

MOSTLY GIRLS

Step 2

After distributing copies of "The Adventures of the Suddenly Grown Up" (Repro Resource 4), instruct the girls to change the name of the character on the sheet from Stan to Sandra (or some other feminine name of their choosing). Also instruct them to change some of the details of the story to make it more applicable to the female character. For instance, rather than being envious of Paul's seventeenth birthday party with his friends, the main character of one of your girls' stories may be envious of her sister's date with her boyfriend on her seventeenth birthday.

Step 4

Provide some blank index cards for a second round of "Grown-Up Concentration." Have your group members work in teams of three or four, writing additional privilege and responsibility cards that include other things that appeal to them about being an adult. After the cards are finished, collect and shuffle them. Spread them out on the floor, and have your group members take turns choosing two cards at a time, trying to find a match. You may want to award a prize to the person who finds the most matching cards.

MOSTLY GUYS

Step 1

Guys might be more comfortable trying to knock each other *off* the board than they would be trying to work together on it. So you may need to alter the activity a bit. Give each contestant a foam rubber bat. Have the contestants face each other on the board. When you say go, the contestants will try to knock each other off the board using only the foam rubber bats. (Contestants may not *touch* each other at all.) The first person to fall off the board—or even touch the floor—loses. If you have time, you may want to make this a tournament, with the winners advancing to the next round until you have a champion ("the chairman of the board"?).

Afterward, point out that when kids begin to mature and take their first steps toward adulthood, it can cause some mighty clashes between them and their parents—if the situation is not handled correctly.

Step 4

Use the following questions to focus on some of the specific *family* responsibilities guys may face in the future.
• **Imagine that you're an adult, with a family and a good job. You work hard forty hours a week. But when you get your paycheck, almost all the money goes toward paying bills, buying diapers and formula for your kid, and paying for car repairs on your mini-van. How do you think you would feel about spending your hard-earned money this way?**
• **Imagine that your son got caught doing something wrong at school. The school principal calls you in for a conference. How would you handle the situation?**
• **Imagine that you're invited to play on your church's Saturday-morning softball team. Unfortunately, your wife works on Saturdays and you have to stay home with the kids—so you can't play. How do you think you'd feel?**

EXTRA FUN

Step 2

Have group members form two to four teams (depending on the size of your group) for a "growing up" relay. Have the teams line up at one end of the room. When you say go, the first person in each line will crawl (like a baby) to the other end of the room and back. Then the second person in line will do the same thing. When all of the team members are finished crawling, the first person in line will then "toddle" (like a toddler)—by taking two steps and falling down, taking two steps and falling down—to the other end of the room and back. When all the team members are finished toddling, the first person will run (like a teenager/adult) to the other end of the room and back. When all the team members are finished running, the first person in line will walk slowly (like an elderly person)—heel-to-toe, heel-to-toe—to the other end of the room and back. The first team to complete all four legs of the relay wins.

Step 5

As you wrap up the session, play a quick game to reinforce the idea of "shocking parents' socks off." Have group members form two teams. Instruct the teams to line up at one end of the room for a relay race. Place two paper bags (one for each team) at the other end of the room. When you say go, the first person in each line will remove his or her shoes, run to the other end of the room, and remove his or her socks. After dropping the socks in the team bag, the person will run back to the team and tag the next person in line. That person will then repeat the process. However, the next person in line may not begin to remove his or her shoes until he or she is tagged. Award a prize to the team that finishes first. [NOTE: You may need to bring some extra socks to the session for sockless group members.]

Step 1

Have group members form teams of two or three. Distribute several magazines, catalogs, and newspapers to each team. Instruct the members of each team to look through the material and find pictures of people that resemble what they think each other will look like as adults. Encourage them to be sensitive as they select pictures (i.e., don't choose pictures of fat, ugly, or grotesque people). Afterward, have the team members discuss what they think each other will be like as adults.

Step 2

Instead of using Repro Resource 4, rent a video of the movie *Big,* starring Tom Hanks. Show several clips from the movie. (You'll need to preview them first to check for offensive language and suggestive situations.) Among the scenes you might want to show are the one in which the young boy makes a wish that he was grown up; the one in which he wakes up the next morning to find he *is* grown up; the one in which he spends the night alone in a run-down, scary hotel; the one in which he's discovered playing in a toystore by the owner of the toy company and given a new position in the company; and the one in which he returns home, a young boy again.

Afterward, discuss the clips, using the following questions.
• **Would you be willing to give up your teenage years to have the kind of life Josh had as a grown-up? Why or why not?**
• **What kinds of things was Josh unprepared for as an adult? Do you think you would be any better prepared for these situations than Josh was?**
• **What kinds of things do you think you need to know before you become an adult?**

Step 2

Rather than distributing copies of Repro Resource 4 to your group members and waiting for them to fill it out, simply read aloud the story on the sheet. Then ask the following questions:
• **How do you think Stan's life will change now that he's grown up?**
• **What kinds of things will he be able to do now that he probably wasn't able to do as a kid?**
• **What kinds of problems will he face now that he probably didn't have to face as a kid?**
• **Has anyone ever told you that you were "trying to grow up too fast"? What did the person mean by that?**
• **Do you think it's possible to grow up too fast? Explain.**

Step 4

You may not have time to wait for each pair of group members to complete the game and solve the puzzle. Instead, you may want to have just one copy of Repro Resources 5 and 6 for all of your group members to use. Tape the "Concentration" game to the wall and have group members form a line in front of it. One at a time, each group member will have a chance to choose two cards. If the cards match, the person gets to keep the cards, attempt to solve the puzzle underneath, and choose two more cards. If the cards don't match, the person must go to the end of the line and wait for his or her next turn. Award a small prize to each person who finds matching pairs of cards and a grand prize to the person who correctly solves the puzzle.

Step 1

If you don't have the lumber required for the opening activity, use masking tape instead. Tape two slim, rectangular strips on the floor (each approximately five inches wide and five feet long). You'll also need to appoint two "floor judges" to observe the pairs and determine whether any part of the contestants' feet touch the floor outside the taped boundaries. Those whose feet touch the floor outside the boundary will be disqualified.

Step 2

Some of your group members may have been forced by circumstances to "grow up in a hurry." Address this possibility with the following questions.
• **How many of you would say you've already taken on adult roles in your family? What are those roles?** (Some of your group members may be responsible for taking care of younger siblings or for shopping and housecleaning.)
• **Why do you have those roles in your family?** (Some group members may come from families in which both parents work long hours. Other group members may come from families in which one parent is absent. Still other group members may have parents who are unwilling or incapable [perhaps due to alcoholism or drug addiction] of taking care of their kids.)
• **Are there any benefits to growing up in a hurry? What are some of the drawbacks?**

Step 2

Separate your junior highers and high schoolers into two groups. Have the junior high group answer this question: **What are three things you're looking forward to when you become an adult?** (Among the things group members might mention are getting a driver's license, buying a car, getting a job, getting married, having kids, getting out of school, making a lot of money, etc.)

Have the high school group answer this question: **What are three things about being a kid that you miss now or probably will miss when you get older?** (Among the things group members might mention are having someone cook and clean for you, not having to make "big" decisions, being able to play with friends without having to be "cool" or self-conscious, feeling safe with and protected by your parents at home, not having to worry about paying bills, etc.)

Getting two different perspectives may help your group members form a more complete picture of the ups and downs of growing up.

Step 4

After the "Concentration" game, distribute the "privilege" cards among your junior highers and the "responsibility" cards among your high schoolers. Have the person with privilege card #1 stand up, read it aloud, and then tell why he or she is excited about having that privilege in the future. (For instance, someone might say, "I'm excited about having a driver's license and driving a car because I'll be able to go where I want, when I want.") Then have the person with responsibility card #1 stand up, read it aloud, and tell why that responsibility is important. (For instance, someone might say, "Following the rules of the road is important because if you ignore them just once, you could ruin your life or someone else's.") Continue until all of the privilege and responsibility cards have been read.

Step 3

Instead of having your sixth graders re-read all of Luke 15:11-20 to find the "bad moves," assign the teams only a few of the verses. Instruct half of the teams to read verses 11-14 and write down better choices for the actions described in those verses. Have the other teams read verses 15-17 and write down better choices for the actions described in those verses. Give the teams a few minutes to work. When they're finished, have them share what they've written. Then discuss as a group how the story might have been different if the characters had made some of the choices suggested by your group members.

Step 5

Before having kids pair up, discuss as a group some things that parents (rather than kids) would view as a step toward maturity. Ask: **Can you name some things that are important to your parents and would show them you're ready to take on more responsibility? What things do your parents say are stressful to them? Do they want more help around the house? Start noticing what your parents think are important and do something about it.**

Planning Checklist

Date Used:

Approx. Time

Step 1: Trading Places _____
o Extra Action
o Small Group
o Large Group
o Mostly Guys
o Media
o Urban
Things needed:

Step 2: Growing Up in a Hurry _____
o Extra Fun
o Mostly Girls
o Media
o Short Meeting Time
o Urban
o Combined Junior High/High School
Things needed:

Step 3: The Prodigal _____
o Extra Action
o Large Group
o Heard It All Before
o Little Bible Background
o Sixth Grade
Things needed:

Step 4: Grown-Up Concentration _____
o Small Group
o Fellowship & Worship
o Mostly Girls
o Mostly Guys
o Short Meeting Time
o Combined Junior High/High School
Things needed:

Step 5: Shock Their Socks Off! _____
o Heard It All Before
o Little Bible Background
o Fellowship & Worship
o Extra Fun
o Sixth Grade
Things needed:

Who's the Boss?

YOUR GOALS FOR THIS SESSION:
Choose one or more

☐ To help kids recognize that most rules make sense when you stop to think about them.

☐ To help kids understand how one member of a family, operating by his or her own rules, can disrupt the entire family.

☐ To help kids identify the reasons behind some of the specific rules in their families and recommit themselves to obedience.

☐ Other _____

Your Bible Base:

Exodus 20:1-17
Proverbs 6:20-22
Ephesians 6:1-3

Checkered Competition

(Needed: Cut-apart copies of Repro Resource 7, buttons)

Before the session, you'll need to cut apart copies of "Championship Checkers" (Repro Resource 7). Make sure you keep the two sections at the bottom of the sheet ("Official Rules for Checkers" and "New-and-Improved Official Rules for Checkers") separate.

As group members arrive, have them form pairs. Distribute a checkerboard from Repro Resource 7 and several buttons (which will serve as checkers) to each pair. [NOTE: You'll need thirty-two buttons for each pair. If possible, give each pair sixteen buttons of one color and sixteen buttons of another color.] Then give one person in each pair the "Official Rules for Checkers" section and give the other person the "New-and-Improved Official Rules for Checkers" section.

Announce that you're going to have a checkers tournament, and that the rules for the tournament are written on the slips of paper you just handed out. Group members must follow the rules when playing.

Have group members begin playing. It shouldn't be long before you start hearing complaints and accusations of cheating. If someone comes to you with a complaint, simply say: **Both of you have your rules— just finish your game.**

No matter how strongly some group members object to the rules, encourage the pairs to complete the games. As they are finishing up, throw one more curve into the process by explaining that there's one rule you forgot to announce: The person with the *fewest* number of buttons left wins the game.

Afterward, point out that the purpose of this exercise was to show how playing by your own set of rules can lead to frustration and chaos.

Say: **The topic of our session today is rules. We are surrounded by rules every day—rules of the road, rules at school, rules of the sports we play, and, of course, the rules our parents give us to live by at home. Today we're going to focus on home rules—the laws you live by at your house.**

Probably few, if any, of you were happy with the way our checkers tournament went. Unfortunately, when everyone plays by his or her own rules, no one can really have a good time. The same can be said for rules at home. When one person in a family thinks he or she can live by his or her own rules, it can be frustrating for everyone else.

My Family's Six Commandments

(Needed: Copies of Repro Resource 8, index cards, pencils)

Ask your group members some of the following general questions about rules at home. Encourage most of your group members to respond to each question.

Who makes up the rules at your house?

Do the same rules apply to all the members of your family? In other words, do mom and dad live by the same rules that the kids live by? What about older or younger siblings?

What's a rule in your house that's changed since you've gotten older? For instance, have your bedtime, chores, or curfew changed?

Distribute copies of "Family Commandments" (Repro Resource 8) and pencils. Have group members write down three "thou shalt" and three "thou shalt not" rules from their families. ("Thou shalt" rules might include something like "Thou shalt take out the garbage on Thursday night." "Thou shalt not" rules might include something like "Thou shalt not get in after 11 p.m. on Saturday night.")

Give group members a few minutes to work. When they're finished, have them compare rules with the people sitting around them.

Distribute two index cards to each group member. Then say: **Sometimes it's tough to understand all the rules our parents think are so great. Look again at the rules you wrote down. Are there any that make no sense at all to you? If possible, choose one "Thou shalt" rule and one "Thou shalt not" rule that you have a hard time understanding the reasons for. Write these rules on your index cards. We'll look at them later to see if we can make some sense out of them.**

Have group members write the two rules on separate index cards. Then collect the cards and save them for later.

O P T I O N S

SMALL GROUP

LARGE GROUP

MOSTLY GUYS

MEDIA

SHORT MEETING TIME

SIXTH GRADE

God's Top Ten Rules

(Needed: Copies of Repro Resource 8, chalkboard and chalk or newsprint and marker)

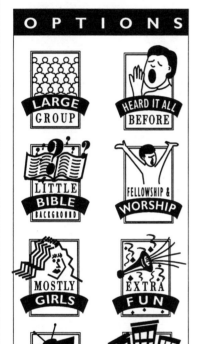
Say: **Perhaps we can get a better understanding of rules by looking at the "top ten" rules God set down for His children.**

Have group members turn in their Bibles to the Ten Commandments passage in Exodus 20. Read aloud verses 1 and 2. Then have group members take turns reading aloud the following passages, as indicated: verse 3; verses 4-6; verse 7; verses 8-11; verse 12; verse 13; verse 14; verse 15; verse 16; and verse 17.

After all the commandments have been read, read aloud verse 18. Then say: **It sounds like the people of Israel were getting a fairly serious message. Imagine a mountain shaking, with smoke and lightning all around, and invisible trumpets blasting. (And you thought your parents were dramatic when they laid down their rules!)**

God obviously wanted to get the people's attention. That must mean the stuff He was saying was pretty important.

Refer group members back to the rules they wrote down on Repro Resource 8. Have them choose from their lists one or two rules that they consider "good," "reasonable," or "useful." Ask volunteers to call out some of the rules they chose. Write the rules on the board as they are named.

Afterward, go through the list of rules, asking of each one: **What makes this a good rule?** You may get a variety of answers, but chances are they will boil down to two criteria.

A good rule does one of two things:

(1) It keeps you from getting hurt, treated unfairly, or ripped off.

(2) It insures that you get something you need.

Say: **We could say that a good rule either protects you or provides for you. Let's look at the top ten rules God gave us in the Bible. Just to make sure everybody understands these rules let me rephrase them in easier-to-understand terms.**

Paraphrase each commandment so that group members understand the concepts clearly. For instance, "You shall have no other gods before me" is simply a command to worship only the one true God. Committing adultery is having a sexual relationship with someone you're not married to. Giving false testimony is telling a lie about someone.

On the board, write the following two headings: "Protects" and "Provides." Then ask: **Which of the Ten Commandments would you say are designed to protect people?** (Commandments like "You shall not murder," "You shall not commit adultery," "You shall not steal," "You shall not give false testimony," and "You shall not covet" are pretty obviously designed to protect people. Commandments like "You shall have no other gods before me," "You shall not make for yourself an idol, "You shall not misuse the name of the Lord," and "Honor your father and your mother" protect people from the *consequences* of these actions.)

Which of these commandments is designed to provide, or make sure people get what they need? ("Remember the Sabbath day by keeping it holy" could be an example of this. Part of keeping the sabbath is resting. Resting on the sabbath gives us the refreshment and energizing we need to face the rest of the week.)

Avoid getting into a long discussion about the pros and cons of the Ten Commandments. That's not the point of the activity. You're simply trying to show your group members that good rules have good reasons behind them.

Say: **Of course God's rules are good; after all, God is perfect. But our parents aren't perfect. What does that say about their rules?** Get a few responses.

Have someone read aloud Proverbs 6:20-22. Ask a few volunteers to comment on the passage. Emphasize the importance God's Word places on parental rules.

Then say: **We've seen how God gives us rules that protect us or give us what we need, and we've seen how a father's rules can do the same for his kids. But what about the rules at your house?**

STEP
4

To Obey the Impossible Rule

(Needed: Index cards from Step 2)

Have group members form teams of two or three. Bring out the index cards you collected in Step 2 and distribute them among the teams.

Explain: **Earlier you wrote down some hard-to-understand rules from your family. Let's take a look at these rules**

again—this time keeping in mind the two purposes for good rules. A good rule is one that either *protects* us from something or *provides* something for us.

Instruct the teams to read their assigned rules and try to figure out the reasons behind each rule. Are the rules designed to protect? Are they designed to provide? Or are there really no good explanations for them?

Give the teams a few minutes to work. Then have each team read a couple of its assigned rules and share its conclusions. It may be helpful to some of your group members to hear their peers spotting the logic in some of their parents' rules.

Afterward, ask: **What can we do about unreasonable rules—those rules that aren't really designed to protect or provide?** Be sensitive here. Some of your group members may really be struggling with unreasonable rules at home. Encourage them to respectfully ask their parents to help them understand these rules. Also encourage them to be open to their parents' explanations and think through what it means to be responsible for a family's protection and provision. Putting themselves in their parents' place may help them accept seemingly unreasonable (and unchangeable) rules.

STEP
5

Obeying Parents = Obeying God

Say: **One of the rules in God's "top ten list" in Exodus 20 had to do with honoring our parents. Ephesians 6:1-3 tells us that the best way to honor our parents is to obey them.** Have someone read aloud the passage.

Then say: **God must think that obeying our parents is a pretty important rule. He put it in there with the other nine biggies. That means when we obey our parents and respect the rules they put down for us, we are actually obeying God.**

Close the session with a time of silent prayer. Encourage group members to tell God how they *honestly* feel about the rules in their families. You might encourage them to start their prayers with a statement like "Dear Lord, sometimes I feel like my whole life is controlled by rules" or "Heavenly Father, You gave me parents who seem so strict compared to my friends' parents. Help me to respect and obey them even when …"

Offer to meet privately after the session with any group member who wants talk about unfair rules in his or her family.

CHAMPIONSHIP
CHECKERS

OFFICIAL RULES FOR CHECKERS

You may move your checkers diagonally one square at a time. When you are next to (on a diagonal) your opponent's checkers, you may "capture" them by jumping over them with your checkers. Failure to obey these rules means you automatically lose the game. Have fun!

NEW-AND-IMPROVED OFFICIAL RULES FOR CHECKERS

Do *not* show your opponent these rules!

The old rules for checkers were boring, so we changed them. Don't worry about only moving diagonally. Move any direction you want—one square at a time. However, on every other turn, you can move to any square on the board. And, by the way, you don't need to jump *over* a checker to capture it. You can jump right on top of it to clear it off the board. Have fun!

FAMILY
Commandments

Step 1

Have group members form two teams to play volleyball. (Kickball or dodgeball would also work, depending on your group members' preferences.) Tape a string or piece of rope between two walls to serve as a net. You could also use tape to mark the out-of-bounds lines. Explain the rules very carefully to your group members. You'll serve as referee for the game. At first, be extremely nit-picking in calling violations. Watch for double hits, carries, illegal serves, close out-of-bounds calls, etc. If possible, make a call on every volley. When group members complain, go to the opposite extreme in your refereeing: don't call anything. If the ball hits out of bounds, count the point. If a person throws the ball over the net, count the point. If the ball rolls under the net, count the point. When group members complain again, discuss as a group the importance of good rules—in competition, as well as in life.

Step 4

Have group members form two teams. One team will line up against a wall; the other team will line up against the opposite wall. On one of the other walls, you'll need to put a container labeled "Good Rules"; on the wall opposite of it, you'll need to put a container labeled "Bad Rules." You'll stand in the middle of the room with the index cards you collected in Step 2. (Use half of the cards for each team.)

When you say go, the first person in line for one team will run to you and grab an index card from your hand. He or she will read aloud the rule written on the card and decide whether the rule is good or bad. Then the person will run to the appropriate container, drop the card in, and run back to his or her team. Continue until you run out of cards for that team. Then have the other team take its turn. Time each team, and award a prize to the winners. Afterward, ask group members to explain their reasoning in determining whether a rule is good or bad.

Step 2

If your group is small, it's likely that your group members know each other fairly well. In that case, they may be comfortable sharing more specific, personal information with each other. Use the following questions to address some of the specific rules in your group members' families.

• **What is your curfew on school nights? What is your curfew on weekends? For those of you who have older brothers or sisters, is their curfew any different from yours? What about younger brothers or sisters?**

• **What is your bedtime on school nights? What is your bedtime on weekends? Are your older siblings allowed to stay up later than you are? Do your younger siblings have to go to bed before you?**

• **What jobs and chores are you responsible for around the house? What jobs and chores are your older siblings responsible for? What about your younger siblings?**

Some of your group members may feel better about their parents' rules if they discover that other kids face the same kinds of rules. However, be sensitive to kids whose parents are obviously much stricter than other parents.

Step 4

If your group is small enough, you won't need to have group members form teams to discuss their families' hard-to-understand rules (which group members wrote on index cards in Step 2). Instead you can discuss them together as a group. Read each rule aloud. Then have your group members vote as to whether they think the rule is good or bad. (Remind them that good rules usually either *protect* us from something or *provide* something for us.) After group members have voted, ask a couple of them to explain their reasoning. If you have differing opinions about a rule, encourage a brief debate.

Step 2

If you have a large group, it might be difficult to have most of your group members respond to the questions about their families' rules. To make this section more personally involving, have group members form teams of three. One person on each team will share with the others about his or her family's rules concerning bedtime—what time he or she has to go to bed on school nights and weekends, what time his or her older and younger siblings have to go to bed, etc. Another person will share with the others about his or her family's rules concerning jobs and chores around the house—who's responsible for what and what happens if jobs don't get done. The other person will share about his or her family's rules concerning curfew—what time he or she has to be home on school nights and weekends, what time his or her older and younger siblings have to be home, etc.

Step 3

Skip the part of the session in which group members call out the rules they wrote down on Repro Resource 8. After you've discussed the Ten Commandments and explained the criteria for a "good" rule (one that either protects you from something or provides something for you), have group members reassemble into the teams of three they formed earlier (if you used the "Large Group" option in Step 2). Have the members of each team look at the rules they wrote down on Repro Resource 8 and decide together which rules are "good," based on the criteria from the session. Then have them brainstorm what might happen if they were to disobey these good rules.

Step 3

For those of your group members who are more familiar with the Ten Commandments than Charlton Heston, you'll need a fresh approach. Try having them "rank" the commandments from 1 to 10, based on how important they think each one is. Distribute index cards and pencils. Have group members decide which commandment is most important, which is second-most important, and so on. Give group members a few minutes to work. When everyone is finished, have each person share his or her list. Pay particular attention to where each person ranks "Honor your father and your mother." Ask several volunteers to explain why they ranked it as they did. Afterward, point out that all of the commandments carry equal weight—none is more important than the others.

Step 4

Probably most of the lessons and sermons your group members have heard on the Ten Commandments have focused on the importance of *obeying* the commandments. So you may want to try a different approach: focusing on the results of not obeying them. Write each of the Ten Commandments on the board. Then, as a group, brainstorm possible results of not obeying each commandment. (For instance, not obeying Commandment #6, "You shall not murder," might result in being sent to prison or executed. Not obeying Commandment #9, "You shall not give false testimony against your neighbor," might result in losing friends.) Pay particular attention to group members' responses for Commandment #5, "Honor your father and your mother." You may want to refer back to these possible results in Step 4, as you discuss the importance of obeying parental rules

Step 3

If your group members aren't familiar with the Bible, you may need to reword some of the Ten Commandments to help group members understand them better. (For instance, "have no other gods before me" means not allowing anything to become more important to us than God.) Use some of the following questions to guide your discussion of each commandment.
• **What percentage of the people in our country would you say obey this commandment?**
• **What is the result in our society of people disobeying this commandment?**
• **How would our society be different if everyone obeyed this commandment all the time?**
Pay particular attention to group members' responses concerning the "Honor your father and your mother" commandment.

Step 4

In abusive homes, certain "rules" may result in physical or emotional harm for kids. Group members who are facing such situations—and who have little Bible background—may misunderstand your emphasis on obedience. They may conclude that obeying their parents involves suffering abuse, and resign themselves to their fate. Or they may decide that you're so "out of touch" with their situation that they can't come to you with their serious problems at home. Emphasize that obeying parents does *not* include suffering abuse. Have each group member write his or her name on an index card. Then ask: **Are you having serious problems with physical or emotional abuse at home? Do your parents have rules that put you in danger, rather than protecting or providing for you? If so, write yes on this card. If not, write no.** Explain that you will meet privately with anyone who writes yes on the card, and that you will do whatever is necessary to help him or her.

Step 3

Write some of the following Scripture passages on the board—Deuteronomy 6:5-9; 7:9-11; 8:1; 12:32; 30:16; Joshua 22:5; Proverbs 13:13; Joel 2:11; John 14:15, 21; 15:14; Ephesians 6:1-3; 1 John 3:24. (All of the passages have to do with obeying God's commands.) Have group members form teams. Instruct each team to come up with a song or chorus that uses the words of one or more of these passages and the tune of a well-known song. (Teams might use tunes from hymns, well-known choruses, or even pop songs.) Give the teams a few minutes to prepare; then have each one perform its composition. To make the presentations more interesting and fun, you might want to distribute kazoos and other toy instruments for the teams to use.

Step 5

As you wrap up the session, have group members form pairs. (It would be good if group members paired up with a friend or someone they know fairly well.) Have group members share *honestly* with their partners how they feel about the rules in their families. If one of your group members is completely fed up with the rules in his or her house, he or she should say so without worrying about what his or her partner will think. After both partners have shared, they should pray for each other's situations.

MOSTLY GIRLS

Step 3

After Proverbs 6:20-22 is read, have group members form teams. Assign each team one or more of the phrases from this passage. Instruct the teams to reword or paraphrase their phrases in a way that would be appropriate for today. For example, in verse 21, "Bind them upon your heart forever" could be reworded to say, "Write them down and memorize them so you will always remember them." After the teams have completed their paraphrases, ask them to read the new versions to the rest of the group.

Step 5

After Ephesians 6:1-3 has been read, discuss as a group our choices in obeying God's rules. Ask: **Does God say that we are to obey our parents only if they are ideal parents? What should you do if your parents aren't obeying God's rules themselves? Does this give you the freedom to choose not to obey them? Why or why not?**

MOSTLY GUYS

Step 1

Most of your guys probably are more interested in basketball than in checkers. So, to more effectively demonstrate the idea of unfair rules, substitute a game of "Pig" (using paper wads and a wastebasket) for the checkers tournament. Give each person a paper wad; then assign the order in which your group members will shoot. In "Pig," if a person makes a shot, the next person must make a shot from the exact same spot. If he misses, he receives a letter (P-I-G). When a person gets three letters, he's out of the game. Play the first round according to the "real" rules; then, add some of your own. Here are some suggestions you might use:
• When a person makes a shot and the next person makes the same shot, give a letter to the first person.
• When a person receives his first letter, tell him that he's out—because you need to "speed up the game."
• When a person makes a shot and the next person makes the same shot, give a letter to the second person—because his shot didn't have the exact same angle as the first person's.
• If a person misses a shot, give a letter to the next person if he doesn't miss his shot in the exact same way.
Afterward, discuss the importance of having "fair" rules.

Step 2

As you discuss the specific rules of your group members' families, focus on gender-related rules. Ask: **Are there any rules in your family that seem to "pick on you" specifically because you're a guy? Are there jobs around the house that you have to do that your sisters don't have to do? If so, how do you feel about that? Are there jobs your sisters have to do that you don't have to do? If so, how do you feel about that? Would you trade jobs or rules with your sisters if you could? Explain.**

EXTRA FUN

Step 1

Open the session with a game of "Follow the Rules." Have your group members form two teams for a relay race. Arrange the teams in two lines at one end of the room. Then explain the rules of the contest and give the teams the signal to start. Your explanation of the rules of the contest is the key to the activity. You'll need to come up with a ridiculous number of rules. As needed, use some of the following suggestions to supplement your own ideas. (You might want to write the rules on the board so group members can refer to them during the contest.)
• Both of your feet may not touch the floor at the same time during the race.
• Your right heel may not touch the floor at all during the race.
• One of your shoelaces must be tied in a double-knot before you race.
• After every third step you take, you must turn and look at me.
• If your shirt has any green in it at all, you must run backward during the race.
Afterward, discuss as a group how having a lot of rules can ruin a person's fun. Ask volunteers to say whether they think they have too many rules to follow at home.

Step 3

Have group members form teams. Instruct each team to write a brief skit, demonstrating what an evening newscast might be like in a society that didn't have the Ten Commandments. In such a society, things like murder, theft, and adultery wouldn't be illegal, or even looked down on. This would make for an interesting newscast. For instance, the anchorperson might report on the murder of an elderly person in his home, and then go live to a correspondent on the scene—for a real-estate report on the suddenly vacant home. And because adultery would probably be widespread, the Hollywood gossip reporter might report on famous couples who allegedly *aren't* having affairs. Use this activity to lead into a discussion on the importance of rules.

Step 2

You'll need to find a recording of the classic Coasters' song, "Yakety Yak." Play the song for your group members. Then have them form teams of three or four. Instruct the teams to rewrite the lyrics of the song so that they reflect the rules a young person today faces. Among the lines group members may rewrite are the following.
- "Take out the papers and the trash—or you don't get no spending cash."
- "Just finish cleaning up your room; let's see that dust fly with that broom."
- "Get all that garbage out of sight—or you don't go out Friday night."
- "You just put on your coat and hat, and walk yourself to the laundromat; and when you finish doing that, bring in the dog and put out the cat."

When all the teams are finished, have each one share (perhaps in song form) its new lyrics.

Step 3

You'll need to bring in several newspapers and magazines. You'll also need to have scissors, tape, and paper available. Instruct group members to look through the magazines and newspapers to find pictures that represent their parents' rules. For instance, if someone thinks his or her parents' rules are extremely strict and well-enforced, he or she might cut out pictures of police officers or army drill sergeants. Have each group member form a collage with his or her pictures by taping them on a piece of paper. When everyone is finished, have each person display and explain his or her collage to the rest of the group.

Step 1

If you're short on time, you may not want to wait for the pairs to finish their "checkers championship." Instead, lead your group members in a game of "Simon Says"—with a twist. Before the game you'll need choose two or three group members to whom you'll show special favor. Explain to these kids (privately, apart from the others) that they don't have to follow the rules in the game. They don't have to wait for you to say "Simon Says" before they make a move—in fact, they don't even have to do what you say when you say, "Simon says." During the game, other group members may complain or try to get away with not following the rules—but don't allow them to. If they don't follow the rules, they're out. Continue the game until only your pre-chosen group members are left. Use the activity to lead into a discussion of the importance of fair rules.

Step 2

Rather than distributing copies of Repro Resource 8 and waiting for group members to fill them out, discuss the topic of family rules as a group. Ask two or three volunteers to talk about "the one rule at their house that affects them the most every day," and explain why the rule affects them so. For instance, someone might say, "Having to do the dishes after dinner before I can watch TV affects me the most, because there are so many dishes that I usually end up missing my favorite shows." After your volunteers have shared, distribute index cards and have each group member write down two rules in his or her family that make no sense to him or her. Collect the cards and save them for later in the session (see Step 4).

Step 3

Have your group members come up with a list of ten commandments (or rules) they believe both children and parents should respect at all times—rules that should not change as children get older. Explain that the purpose of the list is to provide a never-changing basis for parent-child rule making and obedience. Afterward, have your group members decide how they could make this list available to their parents—perhaps through a newsletter, the church bulletin, or some other promotional means.

Step 5

Wrap up the session with the following comments: **One definition of the biblical word "honor" that is often overlooked is "to esteem." Esteeming our parents means not neglecting the God-given responsibility to care for and present our parents with great respect, because of the sacrifices they made for us. Honoring our parents does not suggest that parents are never wrong—or that we have to obey them in extreme or abusive situations. Honoring our parents means doing our best to treat them with the respect they are due for caring enough to raise us—even if they weren't always perfect parents. It also means that when they're too old to provide or care for themselves anymore, we have a responsibility to care for them, to give them esteem and personal *honor*.** Discuss some ways kids can esteem their parents.

Step 1

As much as possible, pair up junior highers with high schoolers for the "championship checkers" tournament. Make sure you give the "New-and-Improved Official Rules for Checkers" slips (from Repro Resource 7) to the high schooler in each pair. When the junior highers begin to complain about their partners' cheating, tell them to be quiet and finish their games. Afterward, give junior highers a chance to vent their frustrations. Use the activity to lead into a discussion of who has the most rules: older or younger siblings. Give both your high schoolers and junior highers a chance to comment on the "fairness" of different rules for different siblings.

Step 4

Ask a couple of high school volunteers to stand up and tell the group about a time when they didn't obey one of their parents' rules—and what happened as a result. If possible, have your volunteers focus on the theme of finding out too late that the rules they failed to obey were meant to protect them. The benefits of this simple exercise may be two-fold: (1) hearing a high schooler talk about the importance of obeying rules may mean more to your junior highers than hearing you talk about it; (2) giving your high schoolers a chance to "share their wisdom" with junior highers may give them more of a sense of responsibility and importance in your group.

Step 2

Before distributing copies of "Family Commandments" (Repro Resource 8), briefly discuss as a group the word "rule." Use the following questions to guide your discussion.
• **What does the word "rule" mean?**
• **What are some other words that might mean the same thing?** (Law, requirement, guideline, etc.)
• **What are some places other than your home where you are guided by rules?**
• **What would happen if there were no rules anywhere?**

Step 4

Instead of distributing the index cards from Step 2 and having group members work in teams, do this activity as an entire group. Write each rule on the board as you read it aloud. Then have group members suggest possible reasons for the rules. After reading and discussing several of the rules, ask group members to suggest ways to modify them to make them "fairer" or easier to obey.

Date Used:

Approx.
Time

Step 1: Checkered Competition _____
o Extra Action
o Mostly Guys
o Extra Fun
o Short Meeting Time
o Combined Junior High/High School
Things needed:

Step 2: My Family's Six Commandments _____
o Small Group
o Large Group
o Mostly Guys
o Media
o Short Meeting Time
o Sixth Grade
Things needed:

Step 3: God's Top Ten Rules _____
o Large Group
o Heard It All Before
o Little Bible Background
o Fellowship & Worship
o Mostly Girls
o Extra Fun
o Media
o Urban
Things needed:

Step 4: To Obey the Impossible Rule _____
o Extra Action
o Small Group
o Heard It All Before
o Little Bible Background
o Combined Junior High/High School
o Sixth Grade
Things needed:

Step 5: Obeying Parents ... _____
o Fellowship & Worship
o Mostly Girls
o Urban
Things needed:

5 Operation Family Storm

YOUR GOALS FOR THIS SESSION:

Choose one or more

☐ To help kids recognize that even the best of families have conflicts from time to time.

☐ To help kids understand that family conflict can lead to family growth if the conflict is handled correctly.

☐ To help kids identify some specific, God-honoring steps they can take to help resolve conflict in their families.

☐ Other _____

Your Bible Base:

Romans 12:10-21
James 4:1-3

Family Blowups

(Needed: Copies of Repro Resource 9, pencils, scissors, blindfold, inflated balloons, straight pins)

OPTIONS

Open the session with the following comments: **We're going to have to change our plans today. Last night I found out that the session we were supposed to study today is on family conflict. Family conflict—can you believe it?! Why would we need a session on family conflict? After all, most of us come from pretty good families, so we don't have to worry about conflict—right?** Probably most of your group members will strongly disagree. If they do, pretend to be surprised.

Ask: **Are you telling me you guys have conflict in your families?** (Yes!) **Well, then I guess we won't have to change our plans today.**

So group members don't feel abnormal for admitting to conflict in their families, assure them that *all* families have conflicts.

Have group members form teams of two or three. Distribute copies of "Family Land Mines" (Repro Resource 9) and pencils to each team.

Say: **Sometimes family life can seem a little like war. Even though most of the time we really do care about our family members, it seems that we get into the biggest blowups over the silliest little things. The sheets I'm giving you have some innocent-looking little disks on them. Actually, they're deadly land mines waiting to explode in your family.** [NOTE: You may need to explain to your group members that land mines are booby-trap explosive devices that are usually buried in the ground. When someone or something passes over the top of a land mine, it explodes, causing massive injury and destruction.]

The scrambled letters you see on top of the mine go into the blanks below. Each of the land mines on your sheet will spell out something that causes "explosions" among family members.

Have the teams compete to see who can unscramble the letters and identify the areas of conflict first. The first team to correctly identify all eight areas of conflict is the winner. Announce that the winning team will be given a "special privilege" later in the session.

Give the teams a few minutes to work. When they're finished, go through the answers one at a time. The correct answers are as follows:

(1) curfew; (2) friends; (3) chores; (4) music; (5) clothes; (6) telephone; (7) homework; (8) allowance.

Cut up two copies of Repro Resource 9 so that you have sixteen individual "land mines." Scatter the land mines on the floor in an open area of the room. Ask for two or three volunteers to attempt to negotiate the "mine field" while blindfolded. Let the volunteers look at the arrangement of the mines before you blindfold them.

To add some excitement to the proceedings, distribute several inflated balloons and straight pins to the members of the winning team from the earlier activity. These group members will follow your blindfolded volunteers through the mine field. Whenever a volunteer steps on a mine, they will pop a balloon. [NOTE: For safety's sake, make sure the balloons aren't popped near people's ears or faces.]

Afterward, say: **Think about the last blowup you had in your family over one of these issues. Which one was it? What happened?** Encourage several group members to share honestly. However, don't allow the discussion to degenerate into a gripe session. Keep in mind some of the stories your group members share. You may want to substitute them for some of the case studies and examples used later in the session.

STEP 2

Two Sides to Every Story

Ask: **What does the expression "There are two sides to every story" mean?** (When two people are involved in an incident or conflict, both of them will have a unique perspective on the event. If you listen to only one person's version of the events, you miss out on the "whole story.")

Point out that family conflicts often occur when one person fails or refuses to see the point of view of another person.

Say: **Let's look at some examples of family confrontations and find out how not seeing another person's point of view can lead to conflict.** Note that the case studies are based on some of the "family land mines" from Repro Resource 9.

• **Susan has a lot of friends at school. Unfortunately, they're not the kind of friends her parents would like her to have. Susan's friends do a little drinking on weekends, and their idea of right and wrong is quite a bit different from**

OPTIONS

LARGE GROUP

MOSTLY GIRLS

MOSTLY GUYS

URBAN

JR. HIGH / HIGH SCHOOL COMBINED

SIXTH GRADE

what Susan's parents believe to be true. Susan's friends are loyal, they like her, and they're really fun to be around. However, Susan's parents have told her she cannot spend time with them.

How might not seeing both sides of the story lead to conflict in this situation? (If Susan's parents don't see Susan's side of the story, they might not recognize some of the good points of her friends. If Susan doesn't see her parents' side of the story, she might not recognize the dangers of spending too much time with her friends.)

• **The rule at Stephanie's house is that no personal phone call can be more than ten minutes long. Her parents have explained to her that when she is with her friends all day long, there's no need to be tying up the family phone for long periods of time in the evening. They've thought about the rule carefully, and to them it makes all the sense in the world. However, to Stephanie it makes no sense at all.**

How might not seeing both sides of the story lead to conflict in this situation? (If Stephanie's parents don't see Stephanie's side of the story, they might not understand how important evening phone calls are for staying in the "information loop" in junior high. If Stephanie doesn't see her parents' side of the story, she might not understand the importance of keeping the phone lines open in the evening.)

• **"Your bed wasn't made, the trash wasn't taken out, and the dog wasn't fed. Get used to the house because that's where you'll be staying all weekend. You're grounded." Josh knew his dad was right about the jobs not being done. But Josh had a good reason for not doing his chores—at least, to him it was a good reason.**

How might not seeing both sides of the story lead to conflict in this situation? (If Josh's dad doesn't see Josh's side of the story, he might not discover that Josh had a legitimate excuse for not doing his chores. If Josh doesn't see his dad's side of the story, he might underestimate the importance of completing his chores.)

• **Lionel's dad is lying in bed staring at the ceiling. His mom is nervously pacing the floor. It's 12:15 and Lionel is nowhere to be found. His curfew is 11:00, and the rule is that if he's going to be late, he must call to say why. His mom is imagining the worst—she's sure there's been a horrible accident. His dad is just plain ticked off.**

How might not seeing both sides of the story lead to conflict in this situation? (If Lionel's parents don't see Lionel's side of the story, they might not discover that he was absolutely unable to call them. If Lionel doesn't see his parents' side of the story, he might not understand how much he upset them.)

STEP 3

Conflict Causes

(Needed: Chalkboard and chalk or newsprint and marker, paper, pencils)

Say: **Families have had conflicts and misunderstandings ever since there have been families. Can you think of some families in the Bible that had conflicts?** (The conflict between Cain and his brother Abel resulted in Cain killing Abel. The conflict between Joseph and his brothers resulted in Joseph being sold into slavery by his brothers. Even Jesus experienced conflict with His parents when He was separated from them at the feast in Jerusalem.)

Write the following statement on the board: "The best families are those in which there is never any conflict." Have group members tell you whether they agree or disagree with the statement.

Then ask: **What causes conflicts in a family?** Chances are group members will mention specific incidents like "My brother comes into my room and takes my stuff without asking" or "My dad changes the channel on the TV to the news when I'm watching a show," etc. Help group members get beyond these specific incidents and into the underlying attitudes like lack of respect for privacy or selfishness.

Point out that a similar question is asked and answered in the Bible. Have someone read aloud James 4:1-3. Then ask: **According to this passage, what causes conflicts?** (Selfishness—people demanding things and doing whatever is necessary to get their own way.)

Say: **Think about the last big blowup you had with your parents. Did selfishness play a role in the conflict? Explain.** If group members are hesitant to talk about their own family conflicts, discuss what role selfishness played in the conflict case studies in Step 2.

Point out that not only does the Bible identify causes for family conflict, it also offers suggestions on how to avoid and resolve conflict.

Have group members form pairs. Distribute paper and pencils to each pair. Instruct the pairs to read Romans 12:10-21 and list at least eight practical suggestions found in the passage for avoiding or resolving conflict.

Give the pairs a few minutes to work; then have them share and explain their responses. For instance, if someone suggests "Be devoted to one another," ask what "being devoted" means. Write the responses on the board as they are named.

Use the following responses to supplement the pairs' answers:

• Be devoted to one another (vs. 10).

OPTIONS

HEARD IT ALL BEFORE

LITTLE BIBLE BACKGROUND

FELLOWSHIP & WORSHIP

MOSTLY GIRLS

MEDIA

SHORT MEETING TIME

JR. HIGH HIGH SCHOOL COMBINED

SIXTH GRADE

- Honor one another above yourselves (vs. 10).
- Be joyful (vs. 12).
- Be patient (vs. 12).
- Share with people in need (vs. 13).
- Practice hospitality (vs. 13).
- Do not be proud (vs. 16).
- Do not be conceited (vs. 16).
- Do not repay evil for evil (vs. 17).
- Do what is right (vs. 17).
- Do not take revenge (vs. 19).

You Say You Want a Resolution

(Needed: Copies of Repro Resource 10, pencils)

Distribute copies of "Solving Conflict Problems" (Repro Resource 10) and pencils. Instruct group members to fill out the top half of the sheet. Explain that the report card is for their eyes only—no one else will see it. Its purpose is to help them evaluate how they're doing in some important conflict areas.

When group members are finished filling out the report card, have them review their answers. Ask them to consider what they could do in these areas to lessen the conflict in their families. For instance, are there any "Never" responses they could improve on? Are there any "Always" responses they could work on eliminating?

Give group members a few minutes to pray silently, committing themselves to working on one area this week—perhaps to be a better listener or to control the expression of their emotions.

As you wrap up the session, refer group members to the bottom half of Repro Resource 10. Point out that these are six steps they could use in resolving family conflicts. Briefly go through the six steps. Encourage group members to discuss the principles on the sheet with their parents.

Close the session in prayer, asking God to help your group members follow through on the commitments they made for resolving conflict in their families.

FAMILY LAND MINES

1

ACME LAND MINES
E R C
Guaranteed to cause family explosions.

_ U F _ W

2

ACME LAND MINES
R D N
Guaranteed to cause family explosions.

F _ I E _ _ S

3

ACME LAND MINES
E R H
Guaranteed to cause family explosions.

_ C _ O _ _ S

4

ACME LAND MINES
M C S
Guaranteed to cause family explosions.

_ U _ I _

5

ACME LAND MINES
T C E O
Guaranteed to cause family explosions.

_ L _ H _ S

6

ACME LAND MINES
L O P N
Guaranteed to cause family explosions.

T E _ E _ H _ _ E

7

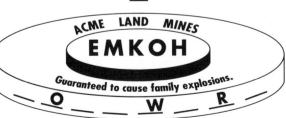

ACME LAND MINES
E M K O H
Guaranteed to cause family explosions.

_ O _ _ W _ R _ _

8

ACME LAND MINES
E W N L
Guaranteed to cause family explosions.

A _ L O _ A _ C _ _

Solving Conflict Problems

	Always	Sometimes	Never
I find it easy to say I'm sorry.			
I find it easy to forgive others.			
I'm a good listener.			
I start arguments or fights for no reason.			
When I feel hurt, I give people the "silent treatment."			
I express my emotions whenever and however I want to.			
I feel sad when I have an unresolved conflict with someone.			

Six STEPS to Solving Conflict

1. Understand that all families have conflict.

2. *Make sure you understand both sides of the story. Ask questions if you don't.*

3. **Be willing to take responsibility for your part in the conflict.**

4. Work together at listing all the possible solutions.

5. *Decide on a solution and work at it together.*

6. *Be willing to forgive or ask for forgiveness if necessary.*

EXTRA ACTION

Step 1

Distribute index cards and pencils. Instruct group members to come up with a list of conflict-causing situations in families. The situations may be as general ("arguments about privacy") or as specific ("My dad barged into my room while I was writing in my diary and read what I was writing") as group members desire. After a few minutes, collect the lists. Then give each person a balloon. You will read aloud the group members' lists. Every time you call out a conflict-causing situation, each group member will blow one deep breath into his or her balloon, and then hold it carefully so that no air escapes. When you read the next conflict-causing situation, he or she will blow another deep breath into the balloon. The first person to pop his or her balloon (by wind power alone) wins. Afterward, discuss how conflict-causing situations, if not handled properly, can lead to "explosions" in families.

Step 4

Ask for three pairs of volunteers. You will give one person in each pair an assignment for the pair to complete. He or she may not tell his or her partner what the assignment is. (Assignments could involve anything from stacking a pile of books in a certain way to cutting out certain letters from a newspaper to form a message.) The members of one pair may not talk to each other at all. They may communicate only through gestures. The members of another pair must wear Walkmans (with the volume turned way up) or earplugs. They may communicate only by yelling. The members of third pair may communicate with each other normally—so obviously it will be easier for them to complete their assignment than it will be for the other two pairs. Afterward, draw a parallel to family communication: It's a lot easier to resolve conflict with your family members if you're communicating normally than if you're not talking at all or if you're yelling at each other.

SMALL GROUP

Step 1

With a small group, you have the luxury of being able to personalize the topic of family conflicts. Have group members form pairs. Instruct each person to share with his or her partner a conflict he or she had with his or her parents recently. Each pair should then choose one of the two conflicts to act out in front of the whole group. The person in the pair who actually experienced the conflict should play himself or herself; the other person should play the parent with whom the conflict occurred. After each pair performs, ask the rest of the group members to share about similar conflicts they've had with their parents.

Step 4

If your group is small and close-knit, they may be willing to share their "grades" from Repro Resource 10. If so, go through the seven statements one at a time, and have each group member share his or her grade for that statement. By doing so, you will help group members see that they are not alone in their problems with parents—that others have similar problems. If you have time, you may want to have group members who "score low" on the same statements get together to discuss ways to improve in those areas.

LARGE GROUP

Step 1

Have group members complete Repro Resource 9 individually. When they're finished, have them form teams of five or six. Instruct the teams to spread out as far away from each other as possible. Each team will cut apart one copy of Repro Resource 9, set up a "mini-mine field," and have its members attempt to step through it while blindfolded (see the description in Step 1). However, team members won't pop balloons when someone steps on a mine. Instead, they will briefly share examples of how the topic of the mine that was stepped on caused real-life conflicts in their families.

Step 2

Have group members form six teams. Assign each team a case study (including the two given below). Instruct the teams to discuss their case studies and answer this question: **How might not seeing both sides of the story lead to conflict in this situation?**
Here are the additional case studies.
• **On Friday nights, Kendra is not allowed to go out until her home-work is done. Usually that's not a problem. Either Kendra doesn't make plans for Friday night or she finishes her homework in study hall. This Friday, however, is the big pool party at Marti's house. And because of a school assembly Friday after-noon, Kendra couldn't get her history report done in study hall.**
• **Lisa hates the way her mom makes her dress. Her jeans are too baggy, her skirts are too long, and her sweaters don't do a thing for her. When Lisa complains, her mom usually has one of two responses: (1) "I don't want you looking 'sleazy'"; or (2) "I can't afford the clothes you want to wear."**
Encourage each group member to participate in his or her team's discussion. Afterward, have each team share its responses.

Step 3

Phrases like "Honor one another" and "Be joyful" probably hold very little meaning for kids who've heard them hundreds of times before. To address this problem, have group members brainstorm very specific, modern-day examples of the commands found in Romans 12:10-21. For instance, for "Be joyful," someone might say, "Be in a good mood in the morning when your mom tries to talk to you during breakfast." Or, for "Practice hospitality," someone might say, "Invite the new kid at school to sit with you at lunch—even though your friends think he's weird and it could cost you your 'status.'" If your group members aren't specific enough with their examples, don't hesitate to tell them and have them try again.

Step 4

Group members who've "heard it all before" are probably used to hearing what *they* need to do (obey their parents, honor their parents, respect their parents, etc.) to bring conflict resolution to their families. As you wrap up this session, give them an opportunity to share what they'd like their *parents* to do to resolve conflicts. For instance, someone might say, "I wish my dad would *listen* to me when I talk, instead of trying to find something wrong with everything I say." After several group members have shared, pray as a group for family-conflict resolution efforts from both sides—kids *and* parents.

Step 1

Kids with little Bible/church background may be reluctant to admit that they have conflict in their families, for fear of being thought of as "unspiritual." Set them at ease at the beginning of the session by sharing some conflicts you had with your parents when you were younger. Also be prepared to explain how you resolved those conflicts and what your relationship with your parents is like now. If possible, bring in some other adults from the church to share about the conflicts they had with their parents. Your goal is to help group members see that conflict between parents and kids is normal—and solvable.

Step 3

Briefly summarize the stories of Cain and Abel (Genesis 4:1-12), Jacob and Esau (Genesis 27), and Joseph and his brothers (Genesis 37; 39–47). Afterward, use the following questions as necessary to guide your discussion of the passages.
• **Why did Cain kill his brother?**
• **Has jealousy ever caused conflict between you and one of your family members? If so, what happened? How was it resolved?**
• **What was the cause of the conflict between Jacob and Esau?**
• **Have you ever been tricked by one of your family members? How did it make you feel? What did you do about it?**
• **How did God use the conflict between Joseph and his brothers to accomplish good?**
• **How might God use the conflict between you and your family members to accomplish good?**

Step 3

Point out that not only does God give us guidelines in His Word for resolving conflict, He also comforts us and gives us strength in the midst of conflict. To help your group members celebrate this fact, lead them in singing the hymn, "Great Is Thy Faithfulness." Focus specifically on the third stanza: "Pardon for sin and a peace that endureth, thy own dear presence to cheer and to guide; strength for today and bright hope for tomorrow, blessings all mine, with ten thousand beside."

Step 4

Rather than having group members pray silently about their "always" and "never" statements on Repro Resource 10, give them an opportunity to share their needs with another group member in a time of fellowship. Have group members pair up (with someone they feel comfortable talking to, if possible). Instruct each person to share with his or her partner one "always" or "never" statement he or she would like to work on in the coming week. After each person has shared, have the partners pray together, asking God to help them follow through on their commitments in the coming week.

MOSTLY GIRLS

Step 2

Divide the girls into two teams for the discussion of the case studies. After talking about seeing both sides of the story, ask the members of Team 1 to put themselves in the place of the kids in the case study. Ask the members of Team 2 to put themselves in the place of the parents involved. Have the teams discuss the emotions their characters are probably experiencing. Then have the teams come together to talk about what might happen *next* in each case study to help resolve the conflict.

Step 3

Have your group members form pairs. Instruct each pair to read Romans 12:10-21 and make a list of the practical suggestions found in the passage. Then ask the pairs to mark three suggestions on their lists that might be the most helpful in resolving the conflicts they face most often. Have the pairs read aloud the three suggestions they marked. List the suggestions on the board as they are named. Then, as a group, choose three items from the board and brainstorm some specific examples of ways a person (specifically a girl) could put those suggestions into practice.

MOSTLY GUYS

Step 1

Use the following questions to get your guys talking about conflict and how they handle it.

How do you usually resolve a disagreement or conflict with …
- **one of your friends?**
- **one of your enemies?**
- **your brother?**
- **your sister?**
- **your father?**
- **your mother?**

Encourage group members to share honestly. Afterward, discuss why they resolve conflicts differently with different people.

Step 2

If your group is made up primarily of guys, the first two case studies (involving Susan and Stephanie) may not be applicable. You may want to use the following two case studies as substitutes.

- **Jeff made the basketball team at school. This is his big chance to be popular. The guys on the team—and the cheerleaders—seem to like Jeff. They invite him to their parties. The problem is that Jeff's parents don't like Jeff's new friends. They say these friends are "too wild"—just because some of them swear and drink a little, and because some of the girls dress a little provocatively. Jeff's parents have forbidden him from hanging around with these new friends outside of school.**
- **One day while Damon's mother was cleaning Damon's room, she noticed one of his heavy metal CDs lying open on his desk. Curious, she read some of the lyrics on the disk— and nearly had a heart attack. She couldn't believe what the songs were saying! Before Damon got home from school, his mother had thrown out all of his heavy metal disks. Now he's not allowed to buy a disk without his parents' permission.**

EXTRA FUN

Step 1

Open the session with a game of "Cup Conflict." Have group members form two teams. Give each team a paper cup, some kind of pedestal or stand (if nothing else is available, a chair would be OK), and several sheets of scrap paper. Each team will place its cup on the pedestal or stand. (Once the game has started, no one may touch the cups at all.) The object of the game is for each team to knock over the other team's cup with paper wads. The paper wads will also serve as "deadly missiles." If a person is hit with a paper wad, he or she is immediately out of the game. As more and more people are put out of the game, strategy for defending your team's cup and attacking your opponent's cup becomes more important. Use the activity as a lead-in to the topic of today's session: conflict.

Step 4

To wrap up this session—and your *Parent Pains* study—invite your group members' parents to join your group for a celebration. Bring in some refreshments (and perhaps even some decorations if you're feeling particularly festive). Organize some games in which parents and their kids can compete together. You'll probably want to include both physical games (like three-legged races) and mental contests (like trivia quizzes). The goal of the activity is for kids and parents to have a good time together. [NOTE: You may want to have some "extra" adults available to team up with kids whose parents couldn't make it to the meeting.]

Step 1

Before the session, you'll need to record several video clips of boxing matches, wrestling matches, fistfights in movies and TV shows, arguments and screaming matches in movies and TV shows, battle scenes from war movies, etc. Have this video playing when your group members arrive. To begin the meeting, have a contest to see who can guess the session topic (family conflict) based on the clues given in the video. Afterward, discuss how family conflict is like and unlike the various kinds of conflict shown in the video.

Step 3

Before the session, you'll need to record several adults (including some of your group members' parents) saying different things that may or may not cause conflict with kids. If possible, have some of the adults use different tones of voice and phrasings in saying essentially the same thing. For instance, one of them might say, "Your room is a pigsty! Get in there and clean it up now!" in a harsh, angry voice. Another might say, "How many times have I told you to clean your room? Why doesn't anyone in this house listen to me?" in a whiny, self-pitying voice. Still another might say, "Would you please clean up your room tonight? We've got company coming tomorrow and I'd like to show off your room" in an even, reasonable voice. Play the recording for your group members, and have them explain which voices/statements might provoke them to conflict and why.

Step 1

When group members are done filling out Repro Resource 9, quickly go through the answers. Then, as a group, brainstorm for each "family land mine" one example of a family conflict having to do with that topic. For instance, for "curfew" someone might say, "My dad grounded me for a week because I was fifteen minutes late getting home from a basketball game. I told him it was because my watch was slow, but he didn't believe me." Skip the activity in which group members try to negotiate the "mine field" while blindfolded. Go directly to the case studies in Step 2.

Step 3

If you're short on time, skip the discussion of family conflicts in the Bible. Instead, focus on the conflict in your group members' families. Ask: **What are the top three things that cause conflict in your family?** Group members may respond with something as general as "bad moods" or something as specific as "My mom doesn't like the clothes I wear." Both answers are OK. Encourage as many group members as possible to respond (even if they can name only one or two causes). Then skip the James 4:1-3 passage and go straight to the discussion of Romans 12:10-21.

Step 1

You might want to change the opening statement of the session to make it more applicable to the urban family situation. You might say something like the following: **We're going to have to change our plans today. Last night I found out the session we were supposed to study is on family conflict—can you believe it? I keep hearing reports on TV and all throughout the media that the urban family is all messed up. I don't know if it's true. Maybe it is! Do you think it's true?** After your discussion, continue with the rest of the activity as planned.

Step 2

The following two situations may be more applicable to an urban setting.

• **Jaleel and his three younger brothers share two beds in the same room. Because his family does not have much money, this has always been the case. But Jaleel is thirteen now and wants his own space to invite friends over. He's mad at his parents because they remind him there is no other room for him to move to. This isn't a good enough explanation for him. How might not seeing both sides of this story lead to conflict?**

• **Shadonda's mother works two jobs to keep a roof over her family's heads. As a result, Shadonda rarely sees her mother anymore. Her mother's asleep in the morning and working at night. Shadonda wants to talk to her mother about some things that are going on in her life, but her mother never seems to have the time. Shadonda feels neglected and robbed of her mother. Her mother keeps promising Shadonda that they will talk, but she never seems to find the time. How might not seeing both sides of this story lead to conflict?**

Step 2

If possible, pair up three junior highers with three high schoolers for a roleplay activity. (Make sure you choose people who feel comfortable performing in front of a group.) Assign each pair a conflict-causing topic such as curfew, allowance, music, clothes, etc. Give each pair a few minutes to come up with a roleplay demonstrating an argument between a parent and a kid, based on the pair's assigned topic. The high schooler should play the parent in the roleplay; the junior higher should play the kid. After the members of each pair perform their roleplays, they should explain to the group why they think their characters were right in the conflict. Use this activity to lead into a discussion of the statement, "There are two sides to every story."

Step 3

Distribute index cards and pencils to your junior highers. Instruct each one to write down a conflict he or she is having or has had with his or her parents. Your junior highers should not, however, write their names on the cards. When they're finished, collect the cards. Ask your high schoolers to come to the front of the room to serve as a panel of "experts" in family conflict. Read each "conflict card" aloud. Then have your high school "experts" come up with a solution for the conflict or advice for handling it correctly—based on their own experiences. Not only will this give your junior highers an opportunity to sound off about the conflicts they're facing at home, it will also give your high schoolers an opportunity to serve as "mentors" to your junior highers.

Step 2

Before the session, you'll need to write each of the case studies and its accompanying question on a separate sheet of paper. (Do not write the suggested answers on the sheet.) Have group members form four teams. Assign each team one of the situations. Instruct the members of each team to discuss their assigned situation and answer the question. Give the teams a few minutes to work. Then have each team read its situation and present its conclusions.

Step 3

For the activity on avoiding or resolving conflict, have your sixth graders work in teams of three or four. Instruct half of the teams to read Romans 12:10-15 and list at least four practical suggestions. Instruct the other half of the teams to read Romans 12:16-21 and list at least four practical suggestions. Give the teams a few minutes to work. Then have the teams take turns sharing their ideas, with each team sharing one suggestion at a time.

Date Used:

Approx.
Time

Step 1: Family Blowups _____
o Extra Action
o Small Group
o Large Group
o Little Bible Background
o Mostly Guys
o Extra Fun
o Media
o Short Meeting Time
o Urban
Things needed:

**Step 2: Two Sides to
Every Story** _____
o Large Group
o Mostly Girls
o Mostly Guys
o Urban
o Combined Junior High/High School
o Sixth Grade
Things needed:

Step 3: Conflict Causes _____
o Heard It All Before
o Little Bible Background
o Fellowship & Worship
o Mostly Girls
o Media
o Short Meeting Time
o Combined Junior High/High School
o Sixth Grade
Things needed:

**Step 4: You Say You
Want a Resolution** _____
o Extra Action
o Small Group
o Heard It All Before
o Fellowship & Worship
o Extra Fun
Things needed:

Custom Curriculum Critique

Please take a moment to fill out this evaluation form, rip it out, fold it, tape it, and send it back to us. This will help us continue to customize products for you. Thanks!

1. Overall, please give this *Custom Curriculum* course (*Parent Pains*) a grade in terms of how well it worked for you. (A=excellent; B=above average; C=average; D=below average; F=failure) Circle one.

           A   B   C   D   F

2. Now assign a grade to each part of this curriculum that you used.

a. Upfront article	A	B	C	D	F	Didn't use
b. Publicity/Clip art	A	B	C	D	F	Didn't use
c. Repro Resource Sheets	A	B	C	D	F	Didn't use
d. Session 1	A	B	C	D	F	Didn't use
e. Session 2	A	B	C	D	F	Didn't use
f. Session 3	A	B	C	D	F	Didn't use
g. Session 4	A	B	C	D	F	Didn't use
h. Session 5	A	B	C	D	F	Didn't use

3. How helpful were the options?
   - ❑ Very helpful
   - ❑ Somewhat helpful
   - ❑ Not too helpful
   - ❑ Not at all helpful

4. Rate the amount of options:
   - ❑ Too many
   - ❑ About the right amount
   - ❑ Too few

5. Tell us how often you used each type of option (4=Always; 3=Sometimes; 2=Seldom; 1=Never)

	4	3	2	1
Extra Action	❑	❑	❑	❑
Combined Jr. High/High School	❑	❑	❑	❑
Urban	❑	❑	❑	❑
Small Group	❑	❑	❑	❑
Large Group	❑	❑	❑	❑
Extra Fun	❑	❑	❑	❑
Heard It All Before	❑	❑	❑	❑
Little Bible Background	❑	❑	❑	❑
Short Meeting Time	❑	❑	❑	❑
Fellowship and Worship	❑	❑	❑	❑
Mostly Guys	❑	❑	❑	❑
Mostly Girls	❑	❑	❑	❑
Media	❑	❑	❑	❑
Extra Challenge (High School only)	❑	❑	❑	❑
Sixth Grade (Jr. High only)	❑	❑	❑	❑

6. What did you like best about this course?

7. What suggestions do you have for improving *Custom Curriculum*?

8. Other topics you'd like to see covered in this series:

9. Are you?
   ❏ Full time paid youthworker
   ❏ Part time paid youthworker
   ❏ Volunteer youthworker

10. When did you use *Custom Curriculum*?
   ❏ Sunday School   ❏ Small Group
   ❏ Youth Group   ❏ Retreat
   ❏ Other _____

11. What grades did you use it with? _____

12. How many kids used the curriculum in an average week? _____

13. What's the approximate attendance of your entire Sunday school program (Nursery through Adult)? _____

14. If you would like information on other *Custom Curriculum* courses, or other youth products from David C. Cook, please fill out the following:

   Name: _____
   Church Name: _____
   Address: _____
   _____

   Phone: (____) _____

                    Thank you!